MIRACLES
CAN BE YOURS

NOEL P. FULLER

About the Cover
(written by designer Craig Faris)

When Dr. Noel Fuller first approached me about doing the cover design for his book, he mentioned that he wanted to call it MIRACLES ALONG THE JOURNEY. From a marketing point of view, I suggested that he change THE to YOUR since the book is about you, the reader, and how God's miracles are yours; eventually it became <u>MIRACLES CAN BE YOURS</u>.

Noel said that he wanted to include the hand of God on the cover and to somehow represent a miracle. NASA had taken a picture of an unusual Nebula, and to my surprise, I discovered that scientists at McGill University in Montreal and at Caltech started referring to the cloud as The Hand of God Nebula. This was the perfect image that I had been searching for to combine with a shot of the Earth taken from space. Also, images from NASA are not copyrighted, because government photos belong to all of us.

I feel that the fact that the Earth "connects" with the MIRACLES along with the nebula, is the nicest part of the entire design. I've been a graphic designer for 38 years, and have found that we pick up a few ideas along the way about what works, and what doesn't work. Sometimes you hit on exactly the right cover ideas by accident, sometimes they seem truly inspired, but perhaps in this case, and in many others, they are all simply miracles.

About the Author, Noel P. Fuller

Noel's first priority is the Lord Jesus, then his family, and then his work. He has a full-time specialty dental practice in Rock Hill, SC. He has a heart for missions and has been on over 50 different foreign mission trips, with numerous different organizations in 9 different countries.

Raised in Greenville, SC, he completed high school, college, and dental school in Charleston, SC. He was president of the student body at the College of Charleston and received the prestigious C. Norwood Hasting Award for honor at graduation in 1970. At the Medical University of South Carolina he received numerous awards at graduation and served 2 years with the 3rd Marine Division, receiving many athletic awards and the Navy Achievement Medal. He completed his specialty endodontic training at the Ohio State University, publishing his study on pain control, taught at the College of Dental Medicine in the Medical University of South Carolina, and began his private practice in Rock Hill in 1980. Dr. Fuller is active in Rock Hill Bible Fellowship Church and numerous professional organizations. He still makes time to run a marathon every few years, and enjoys hunting, fishing, and playing golf. He is married to Pam and their first-born son lives with his family in Charlotte, NC. Their second-born son currently resides in Wilmington, NC.

Acknowledgements

The first person I would like to acknowledge is the Holy Spirit. His motivation and direction were truly supernatural, as He guided the arrangement of chapter after chapter throughout this project, and His persistence was gently effective; furthermore, He was always available. Thank you for allowing me to be transparent in Chapter 13. I pray that HE will motivate many more to find true freedom as they do the same. And then, when I thought I was finished, He said, "I'm not done;" hence, the addendum.

Maureen Angell is one amazing editor, not only superbly skilled, but an encouraging gem of a lady. She has years of experience and works with speedy efficiency. Truly my kind of person, for when she gets to work, she gets the job done rapidly with excellence. Our little joke was "Ain't no piddlin' here."

Craig Faris is a blessing to be around, and is a distinctively natural teacher who loves precision. That is quite obvious by his cover story; thank you for a glorious cover. He is an excellent writer in a different league than my dental mindset.

Pam is the love of my life. She is filled to overflowing with MERCY and her kindness is palpable. She was very patient with my trips around the world, as well as my many trips alone to my man cave to write this book which, amazingly, took just over a month. Her laughter is truly filled with joy and she has been a blessing to me for almost 40 years now. Thank you, Lord, for enabling her to hang on during our ups and downs of The Wild Ride, which WAS the original title for this book.

I thank several of my dental colleagues who challenged me to write a book, after reading my quarterly letters over the years. Also, the numerous patients who listened to my miraculous encounters while we were waiting for root canal anesthesia; many of them encouraged me to "write it down." Thank you for giving me the challenge.

And last but not least, my dear Pastor Lalo from Guyana and Pastor Ken from Rock Hill who have always been tremendous sources of encouragement, correction, and challenge. You are both truly men of God, and you are appreciated more than you will ever know this side of Heaven.

The young Fuller family.

Copyright © 2017 by Noel P. Fuller

All rights reserved. This book or any portion thereof may not be reproduced or used in any manner whatsoever without the express written permission of the publisher.

All rights reserved.

ISBN 979-8-868-5018-1-4

TABLE OF CONTENTS

About the Cover II
About the Author, Noel P. Fuller III
Acknowledgements IV
Introduction IX
Chapter 1 – Obey Even if You Can't Afford It 1
Chapter 2 – A New Birth and Rebirth 8
Chapter 3 – Future Preparation 14
Chapter 4 – Sudden Calamity 24
Chapter 5 – Small Words–Big Impact 29
Chapter 6 – Divine Appointments 35
Chapter 7 – An Amazing Man 41
Chapter 8 – Up Close and Personal 49
Chapter 9 – Horsley Green 61
Chapter 10 – Family Evangelism Excursion 68
Chapter 11 – Another Divine Appointment 72
Chapter 12 – To Russia with Love 79
Chapter 13 – Subtle Deception and Distraction 86
Chapter 14 – Bass Ackwards to Kenya 96
Chapter 15 – London to Nairobi and Beyond 102
Chapter 16 – Clean Air and Real Christianity 108
Chapter 17 – Another English Colony 116
Chapter 18 – The Garden of Eden 121
Chapter 19 – Rainy Nights 128
Chapter 20 – How About You? 134
FREEDOM AND VICTORY! 139
Ann and Calvin – Dec 19, 2009 143
Addendum for Future Contemplation 144

Introduction

In 1982, a good friend of mine told my wife, shortly after we were married, "If you can hang on, it will be a wild ride." Little did Pam know that those words would be prophetic, and God has certainly given her the grace to hang on, as we have seen numerous hardships turn out to be miracle after miracle: financial, emotional, physical, and medical. Following are some short stories about our family, many of my *foreign mission trip experiences*, and our journey together over the past 35 years; our prayer is that they will give you COURAGE for the commitment and perseverance that everyone needs in order to HANG ON during the brief journey we call life on earth.

We all experience miracles from time to time, but sometimes we do not recognize them because our perceptions are our reality; the problem is that most of us have *poor or faulty perceptions*, and we are bound by an *erroneous view of time and pain*. The Bible tells us that "we are like vapors that appear for a little while and then vanish away" (James 4:14), and also talks about "our momentary, light afflictions" (2 Corinthians 4:17); yet we really think that a life span of 80 or 90 years is long, and our pain is intense. However, our life is short and our afflictions are miniscule compared with the eternal life and spiritu-

MIRACLES CAN BE YOURS

al/emotional/physical agony of our Lord. Yes, *He is everyone's Lord*; it is just that most people don't recognize that fact yet.

The original miracle, as far as the human race is concerned, was when God said, "Let us MAKE man" (Genesis 1:26). God did not speak us into being like everything else; He made us, and that makes us special. The amazing reality is to know that the great I AM actually made us, all of us, in His infinite wisdom *before He created the foundations of the earth*. Can you even imagine? Yes, God is *present tense* throughout eternity; our finite minds cannot begin to comprehend that kind of reality. Ironically, we have quantum mathematicians and physicists trying to understand time, create their own big bangs, black holes, and various Towers of Babel, trying to play God. Mankind will NEVER be able to understand or comprehend who God is, how He works, nor His timetable, but we CAN know the miracle of His grace. Such a simple word, and yet packed with supernatural benefits. I like the acrostic GRACE – <u>G</u>od's <u>R</u>iches <u>A</u>t <u>C</u>hrist's <u>E</u>xpense! Yes, He said, "It is finished" because He has already done it.

I dedicate these writings to the Lord, who transformed my life when I was 32 years old, my wife, our wonderful sons, grandsons, and special friends all around the world. We pray that you will receive these little vignettes with contemplation, and ultimately, receive His marvelous grace on a *personal level*, if you do not already *know Him intimately*. If you are at that point in your spiritual walk, my challenge is to obey the Lord's "Final Command." Do you know what it is? Our blessings are contingent upon our obedience! Please read the proof of that fact in the following chapters.

— Noel Fuller

CHAPTER 1
OBEY EVEN IF YOU CAN'T AFFORD IT

I began my private dental practice in October, 1980 in Rock Hill, SC; even though the bank owned it, it was MINE. Everything was mine, and my trinity was me, myself, and I, as I had been brainwashed in good old humanism in college. Just before an amazing salvation encounter with the Lord in December of 1980, I met a beautiful lady who swept me off my feet, and looking back on it, I'm glad we did not start dating right away; I would have messed up AGAIN. Yes, my first marriage in 1978 ended in her walking away after several months, and for good reasons – I was hooked on marijuana and got high every night. Even though I was a professor at the Dental School in Charleston, SC, I was a MESS; everyone knew it but me!

However, the Lord can break down any and all barriers whenever He wants, and the phrase *Jesus is Lord* became a reality for me on my birthday, 1980 – what a gift! I was truly set free, and could say "no" to the bondage of my addiction. More importantly, I had a desire to know Jesus more intimately, and I began my *adventurous study* of the miraculous Word of God. Then when my beautiful lady, Pam, came back into the picture in December of 1981, I was a new creation, and I was part of the Lord's team instrumental in her salvation encounter with

Miracles Can Be Yours

Christ. We started dating, and a few months later, I asked her to marry me while watching the Masters Golf Tournament on TV. We were in her brother's apartment, cuddled up on a couch, and it went something like this: "I have a good idea: I think we should get married." Pam said, "That IS a good idea," and we married a month later!

There is no sense in *dilly dallying around* when you know everything is RIGHT. That little phrase, *dilly dally*, became a hallmark of our future adventures, as we normally did things without piddling, another Southern expression. I guess every couple has their own little personal expressions that define their activities. Yes, we came out of the choir after church, changed clothes, proclaimed our personally designed Scriptural vows, ate some cake, got into my little truck with my bird dog, and pulled our little boat named "Honey Moon" to Lake Jocassee. We were like Adam and Eve for 3 days camping by a beautiful waterfall, and did not see anyone except the owners of the little store where we got our food each day. Then we went to Myrtle Beach for 3 days, and we don't know if our first son was a fresh water or salt water conception, but the Lord was working quickly to start our family. Yes, we had a brand new marriage, a baby on the way, a new dental practice, and we lived in the little house that was home for my dental office as well, to save some money. Yes, I was a dental specialist, but I was strapped with student loans, as well as business and equipment loans pressing; most people thought I was well off financially, and I received several financial investment invitations.

Then another invitation came from Pete, a man in my church: "The Lord wants you on our team going to Peru to help build a Bible translation center." I was polite and asked for details. It would involve a 15-hour drive to Miami, direct flight to Lima, Peru, overnight in the Wycliffe Center, an

1 – OBEY EVEN IF YOU CAN'T AFFORD IT

8-hour bus ride to Huánuco in the Andes Mountains, joining a construction team for a week, and coming home. It would be a 10-DAY trip, and I would need to "raise my own support," whatever that meant. I was still trying to establish referring dentists to send root canal patients to my new dental office, so I said, "I'm in some major debt right now, and there is no way I could leave the office for 10 days." I thought that would be the end of his request, but Pete asked me an important question, "Have you ever trusted the Lord for anything other than your salvation?" I asked him what he meant, so he asked another question, "Don't you think the Lord can manage your office and your finances?" I started to say NO, but I said, "I guess so." He wisely said, "Well, you pray about it and I'll get back with you."

Sure enough, the next week at church he asked, "Are you on go? I know God wants you on our team." Before I could say "no," he said, "You keep praying about it." I think he knew that my prayer life consisted of prayer before meals and a little night time quickie – he was right! The following week he asked if my wife and I could join him for lunch with another couple that was *on go*. So we all went to a great little buffet lunch place, and the topic of conversation was *an awesome trip*. Hal was really neat and Jean was beautiful; they had no children, but wanted several, and they congratulated us on our pregnancy. They were excited about Peru, and encouraged me to go. It was going to be their first mission trip, too. I kept thinking, "No Way."

My dad had been a world traveler during his 33 years in the military, and our family was the recipient of that benefit on several occasions in my younger years, so the prospect of a visit to Peru was intriguing, for sure. Dad died when I was a senior in college, and before he got really sick, I remember him telling me, "Seeing the world is like opening an oyster,

Miracles Can Be Yours

enjoying all the colors inside, and tasting the unique flavor; be sure to enjoy it when you can." I had seen the Appalachian Mountains, but never the Andes, so I began to think this trip might be possible. Other than my own years in the Navy, when I had seen much of the Orient, I had done very little travel; life was occupied with dental studies. Furthermore, I did not remember many of the Orient details because I was floating high on marijuana most of the time.

So, other than the fear of leaving the office for 10 days, I was beginning to have some peace about going to Peru. Even the demonic forces were involved in my thoughts, telling me that I would not be able to handle the temptation of Peruvian hash – supposed to be *good stuff*. I was committed to saying "NO" to that tool of Satan, and I had been successful thus far, even though the temptation to *get high* was daily at my door of opportunity; it was just a phone call away. Yes, it had not taken me long to find the *wrong friends* after I had moved to Rock Hill. I began to pray like I never had before, asking the Lord, "Do you want me to go?" Prior to that, I had always been in charge of determining what I would do and when I would do it; that is probably why I had failed in marriage, and that failure had been an ever-present pain in my heart. Marriage is certainly a TWO-way street, and it certainly is wise to be in the same lane; that requires open, transparent, communication – and agreement.

So what did I do? I asked my new bride how she felt! A seminar that I had attended on Basic Life Conflicts had instructed me wisely: "Don't ask your wife what she *thinks*; ask her how she *feels*." As I remember, she was a little hesitant, but she said, "Whatever you really want." Yes, the joy of being a newlywed! I kept praying, and the Lord gave me peace, so I told Pete, our trip leader, that I was on go. He wisely had me over to his home on a few occasions for a Bible study on

1 – Obey Even if You Can't Afford It

spiritual warfare – he knew what was going on in my mind. I did not know that he knew, but looking back on how all this took place 34 years after the fact, *He Knew!* Yes, it is an amazing little contemplative analysis to *look back on major events* to see *how they happened*; my conclusion now is *God makes no mistakes,* and He is the very present Lord, as 10 years ago and 10 years into the future are *Right Now* for Him. That is why He is *I AM*, and when we pray in accordance with His will, we can thank Him for having received it, even when it has not happened yet. The key is praying *according to His will!*

Months flew by and August was upon us – we were to leave in just a few weeks! My receptionist who was also my office manager asked me, "Dr. Fuller, what should we do about the bills due on the first of the month?" We had about $600.00 in my business account, and over $3,000 due on the first of the month with *no production* until my return in early September. I asked her to send out billing statements early, and told her, "I'm trusting God, but if nothing comes in, I'll just borrow more money when I get back." The bank had been used to me coming by. Yes, it was late August when we packed up Pete's van for the long haul to Miami – 15 hours on the road to *save money*. We were all on a faith trip financially, and I was leaving my new, pregnant wife behind.

Lima, Peru was a gorgeous city, a jet set stopover like Acapulco, Mexico, with clean streets, flowers everywhere, 30-foot poinsettia TREES, beautiful old Catholic churches, and a nice Wycliffe Center for our much-needed overnight, before our long bus ride to Huánuco – 6,000+ feet into the Andes mountains. Well, the bus ride was a trip in itself with no guard rails and huge drop-off cliffs in several places; I did lots of praying. The first morning in Huánuco, I went out for a little jog, as I was an avid runner, only to pull up short because of the altitude; I walked back to our construction project with lots

MIRACLES CAN BE YOURS

of strange looks from the local people. I remember saying "good morning" to several men, with blank looks in return, so it hit me: these people have never heard the English language! "Buenos Dias" was much more appropriate and acceptable. That was my first lesson in foreign missions – learn how to say hello in *their language*, and that alone can open doors. I was invited to have coffee after the correct greeting; I didn't know much of what they were saying, but the door opened!

Perhaps the most common question that people in non-tourist underprivileged areas ask is "Why are you here?" The dream of most people there in Huánuco was to come to America, so when I showed up in their area, they were very inquisitive. That certainly created several witnessing opportunities for this bald-headed man, and I had the privilege of leading my little teenage cement-mixing handy helper to the Lord, which set my evangelistic heart on fire, and I became an excited *seed planter* for the Lord.

So, the fruit of my obedience to the call of missions, when it seemed financially foolish, was definitely a *burning desire* to be more involved in foreign missions, and the fruit for Hal and Jean was the first of FIVE children – yes, Jean came home pregnant. Furthermore, my unexpected miracle was more money in the business account than before leaving on the trip, and ALL of the immediate bills had been paid on time. Yes, the Lord *is worthy to be completely trusted* to take care of ALL matters!

Life is certainly a learning experience, and the best possible education comes from the Lord, as we learn to listen to Him, and obey Him. I love the simple refrain, "Trust and obey, for there is no other way to be happy in Jesus". In 2015, I was privileged to complete my 52nd short-term trip, and have learned that the best thing to give the Lord is your time; it is your *most important* asset. Joyfully giving 10% of your finances

1 – Obey Even if You Can't Afford It

is an essential step of faith, but giving 10% of your TIME reaps rewards that one cannot even purchase: loving relationships, a vibrant appreciation of simple things, and inner peace – those things are not for sale, because the price has already been paid, and they are available only through a personal relationship with the one who paid it. Unfortunately, most people are *still trying to earn or buy* the gifts that are readily available from the Lord. I have had the bonus of excellent health, without any pharmaceutical assistance, a great family, and JOY! Please check out the next chapter, where you can receive two miracles for the price of one!

Chapter 2
A New Birth and Rebirth

The marriage ceremony and honeymoon is certainly an exciting time for a couple; however, there is nothing more exciting a couple can experience than the birth of their children. Although it was almost 33 years ago at this writing, I can vividly remember all of the details that led up to the birth of our first child, just like it was yesterday. Somehow the joyous events of life have a way of permanently etching into our recall system of neurons the ability to bring them to remembrance at any time we choose. Such is the case now, so please let me share them with you.

The hormonal and physiologic changes that take place during pregnancy are an amazing prelude to the *magical adrenalin rush of the birth.* Everything from a change in the sense of smell, pregnancy glow, the unexplainable nausea, episodes of laughter, and other mood swings that a husband is totally unprepared for, and *then the labor pains that are totally unpredictable.* Arriving home from work on a Friday afternoon, just a week before her due date, my anxious Pam said, "I've been having some pains." "How bad are they?" asked a logical husband. "OH, there goes another one!" Let's see, was that the question I asked? So I thought I'd try another one: "How frequent are they?" Pam said, "I don't know – just call the doctor" with a

2 – A New Birth and Rebirth

voice of urgency. "How long has this been going on?" Still no answer, so I picked up the phone – that is back when we had real phones with curly cords. I left a message with the doctor's nurse, "My wife is having pains, please call ASAP," and proceeded to get a shower. In the middle of the shower, I heard, "Oh, that is a bad one," so I quickly estimated maybe 4 minutes since the last pain, jumped out of the shower to dry off, and the phone rang, so I ran to the phone with no clothes on and got fussed at by guess who. Good, it was the doctor asking, "How frequent are the pains?" – "She estimates they are about 4-5 minutes apart" – "Get her in here; I'll be in the office." We were in Rock Hill, SC, and the doctor's office was about 40 minutes away in Charlotte, NC, so I told him that it may be 45 minutes. "Come on, these are not Braxton Hicks." As I was putting on clothes, another pain came, and I was thinking, "We may have a baby in a '57 Chevy – what a great story!"

So we went to the doctor, and he took one quick look and said, "Get over to the hospital, we're having a baby, I'll call them." Fortunately, the hospital was just a block away, and they were ready for us. The pain was really coming now, as Pam was in transition. I said, "Take some breaths," and gave Pam a couple of breaths to lead her; we did great in our Lamaze classes just weeks earlier. Well, Pam got sick – throw-up sick – so I knew she was in bad pain. I said, "Breathe, Pam," and she said, "Get a doctor!" So I left the birthing room, ran to the nursing station to request an epidural, which was *on the way*. I watched someone put a long needle into her back, and Pam did not flinch; minutes later the pain was gone, but the epidural turned out to be a spinal, and when our OB doctor arrived he was upset. He gave Pam some pain medicine for her headache, and something to stop the contractions, and told me, "They will take care of her; she'll be fine for the night; we'll have the baby in the morning." We both slept off and

MIRACLES CAN BE YOURS

on, and Pam was worn out. Up early to the birthing room, and sure enough, at 7:25 on Saturday morning, with two nurses pushing and our doctor pulling with forceps, our healthy baby arrived, and it was the most exhilarating feeling of electricity running through my body, as I saw my first son. His face was a little bruised from the forceps delivery, but he smiled as he heard my voice. How amazing that he had been listening to me since he was 20 weeks old! Yes, hearing is the first sense to develop, right after the heart starts beating, and hearing is the last sense to go before we die. Even more amazing is that faith comes by hearing.

Financial security is a great concept, and insurance companies help provide that; however, they love their *mice print in contracts*. After spending a couple of hours with Pam and our little bundle of joy, I was asked to go to the business office at the hospital, and they broke the news to me that *Pam had missed her 9-month waiting period on our maternity coverage* by just 5 days; yes, that meant we had *NO coverage for the birth of our son*! I should have added her to my policy right after we were married, but that was the last thing on my mind during our honeymoon, so I added her right after we got home from the beach. We were not even thinking about conception, but that natural phenomenon does not require thought!

So, how much is the hospital bill? If we go home on Monday afternoon, which the hospital recommended, the total would be $3,200. That was a lot of money for me, and I did not have it. Well, what does a Christian man do? He prays, "Help me, Lord," and he asks his church to pray on Sunday morning. Then, as a businessman, I called my bank on Monday morning requesting a check for $3,000 made out to Presbyterian Hospital, applied to my account, so I could bring my wife and son home from the hospital that afternoon – "No problem," said the bank officer, as he knew my credit limits

2 – A New Birth and Rebirth

very well. So what does God do? He has the mailman come into the office just before lunch to deliver *23 insurance checks totaling $3,206.* I was overjoyed, called the bank to cancel the check, put a wicker basket in my '57 Chevy, and headed to Charlotte with my American Express card to bring home the family. When Pam heard the story about the bank and the mail delivery she said, "He is right on time!" Yes, the Lord is rarely early, but He is never late when it comes to answered prayer; that is, unless the answer is NO or WAIT, and we need wisdom to discern that. We are supposed to give God thanks and praise no matter what. Remember the three lads in the furnace? (Daniel 3:16…)

Now we fast forward to 2014, to Buff Bay, Jamaica, when this same dad is speaking to a 59-year-old Rastafarian named Franklin (Fire), and has the blessing of witnessing a different kind of birth – a rebirth. Fire has been selling coffee since 1995 to the missionaries who visit the Buff Bay Mission House, and he is well known for his handshake and his hair, which goes to the floor. For the previous 3 years this same dad, known in Buff Bay as "Doc," had been sharing with Fire about the Christian life compared to another lifestyle, the world of marijuana, music, and women – a tempting false god. Also, there were discussions about the Lake of Fire and who is going there, heaven and who is going there, and how we can know where we are going. So Doc invites Fire to spend a week in South Carolina in his home, and offers to pay all of his expenses. All Fire needs is a passport and a visa, so Doc offers Fire a $50 bill with the request, "Get your passport, and let Pastor Allen know; then I'll send a letter saying I'll sponsor you to the US, which will allow you to get a visa. Then I'll send you the money for your airfare." Fire asked, "Doc, why you wanna be so good to me?" "Fire, I don't want to see you go to the Lake of Fire." So Fire takes the money and shakes Doc's hand.

Miracles Can Be Yours

Back in the states the word Doc receives from Pastor Allen about Fire's passport was, "He is working on it." The following year Doc is back with another team, and sure enough, Fire comes to get new coffee orders. Doc asks, "Were you able to get your passport?" "Na, man, need to get a birth certificate first, and we have problems here;" "That's OK, just keep working on it." Then Doc is able to remove one of Fire's bothersome teeth, painlessly to Fire's surprise, later that week. The following day Fire comes by with his bags of Blue Mountain coffee for our team – eight men in 2015, with the topic of "spiritual gifts" to share with the men of Buff Bay. Doc buys 10 bags of coffee, and Fire shakes his hand, and there is no mention of the $50 bill given to Fire the previous year. "How is your gum healing, man?" asks Doc; "Man, that was summin els – neverhurt an donhurt now." Jamaicans can speak realfas, man. Doc asks, "You got a few minutes, Fire? Let's talk about grace." So they sit down and have a good conversation about mercy and GRACE – God's Riches at Christ's Expense – Fire says he understands. Then some of the team share a good laugh with Fire about some of the things men do – eating too fast is one of them. Yes, laughter is good medicine. As Fire leaves the Mission House, Doc says, "Hope to see you tomorrow evening – we leave Saturday morning." Fire says, "Ya, man."

The following day, Fire comes in with a nice looking lady, introduces her, and says, "Doc, she's a Christian." Many people have been praying for Fire over the years, and about that time the Holy Spirit takes over; Doc says, "Fire, I'll tell you the truth, you won't be able to keep this beautiful lady unless you can pray with her, and you won't be able to pray very effectively if YOU are not a Christian." Fire says, "Really, man!" Doc says, "Fire, if I were to give you a $100 bill, what good would it do you if you did not receive it?" "What chu mean, Doc?"

2 – A New Birth and Rebirth

"I mean, if you didn't put it in your pocket, what good would it do you?" With a disappointing look, Fire says, "No good." Doc says with all sincerity, "Well, Fire, I'll tell you the truth, Jesus is the same way, you may have Him in your head, but if you don't receive Him into your heart, and live for Him, He can't do you any good, and you can't be a Christian without receiving His forgiveness." Doc can see a light come on in Fire's eyes, so he says, "You want to pray right now and ask Him to forgive you for your sins, and ask Him to come live in your heart?" Without hesitation, Fire says, "Ya, man!"

So right there in the Mission House, on a beautiful Jamaica evening, with his lady by his side, Fire repeated a simple little prayer confessing his sin, asking for forgiveness, and asking Jesus into his heart. REBIRTH! Doc thought Fire was going to shake his hand, but he grabbed him with a big hug, and would not let go; Doc could feel his shoulder getting wet as Fire's tears began to flow. Then he hugged his lady and several of the men in the meeting room. Doc had almost the same electric thrill as at the birth of his first son.

By the way, our little son was just 5 years old when he walked out of the bathroom one morning and said, "Mommy, I just asked Jesus to come into my heart, and He did." Pam was overjoyed and called Dad at work. Yes, the FIRST birth and the SECOND birth, rebirth, or being born again, are miraculous events. Have you been born again – Is Jesus in your heart, controlling your life, and are you living for Him?

Chapter 3
Future Preparation

You may remember back in Chapter 1 that I came home from Huánuco with a burning desire to be involved in foreign missions, and that fire was certainly alive and well 6 months later. I was looking forward to the invitation to go back for the completion of their translation center. Hal and Jean were occupied with a new baby as we made final preparations for our departure, and this time we flew out of Charlotte, NC to avoid the long drive to and from Miami. I was really looking forward to seeing my little helper from the previous year who gave his heart to the Lord on the final day of our trip. Sure enough, he was growing physically and spiritually, and had learned to speak English with ease. In fact, he amazed me, as he quoted the first two chapters of the Gospel of John word perfect. I had left for him my little cassette recorder with a couple of praise tapes, and a recording I made for him of the Book of John, encouraging him to listen to it. Unbeknownst to me, he had been memorizing it word perfect, with my Southern accent intact. He thought I had spoken it by memory, so he was doing the same! Often I struggle with Scripture memory, especially now that I am 67, but I was proud of the fact that I had memorized the third chapter of James, trying to get a handle on my crazy tongue. It would unexpectedly fly

3 – F‍UTURE P‍REPARATION

off the handle, uncontrolled, with unacceptable volume more frequently than I intended, especially when I was angry. One would have never known that I was a Christian! I did a lot of praying about that, and gradually, the Lord began to set me free, but I would still revert back to the old nature, especially with people I loved – what a sad state of affairs. I learned that, back in the Old Testament days, in order to be a rabbi, memory of the Torah (the first five books of the Bible) was encouraged and often required! Is that not unreal? That sure put a lid on my pride.

So, back to Huánuco in 1983, the project coordinator put us to work right away. Knowing that I was a dentist, he figured I must be good with my hands, and asked me if I'd be willing to lay floor tile. "Sure, I'll be glad to," I responded, but I should have added, "if someone can show me how." He gave me a tub of the black tar, or whatever you call that adhesive, a fancy trowel, and showed me the room where a case of tile was waiting. A couple of chalk lines had been snapped across the floor, but in my wisdom, I started in one of the corners, and I had that black stuff all over my hands and shoes in no time. Our coordinator came by and said, "Whoa, you are supposed to start in the middle of the room on the chalk line" as he picked up one of the tiles and placed a *little bit* of the adhesive down on the floor with his own trowel, and laid the tile perfectly on the two lines. "Start right here, OK?" He was working in another room, and fortunately came back to check on me about 10 minutes later; I had done what I thought was a good job with the tile circled neatly in place in the center of the room, but there was adhesive all over the tiles, and me. I did not know that one was supposed to do one quadrant at a time, with NO excess adhesive, so he asked me if I could paint. "Yes, I love to paint," and he asked if I could keep the paint off me. He was upset. I cleaned up and started painting, very meticulously!

Miracles Can Be Yours

I often wondered what went on at the leaders meeting that afternoon – maybe they did not like the way I painted – because after dinner, Pete asked me if I would like to go with him to a remote facility that had not had a dentist in over 2 years, and help some people who had been in pain. If so, we would fly there in a small plane in the morning, and they would need to radio the pilot right away. My response was, "Sounds exciting." Little did I know that dentistry in primitive areas was going to be right up my alley in future years, but God knew, and little did Pete and I know that we would be up for the airplane ride of our lives on the way back!

The next morning after breakfast we had a group devotional and prayer time, and Pete and I were off in a taxi for the airport, 20 minutes away. We had flown into Huánuco just the day before, and now we were leaving again. As we were waiting, the commercial jet that we flew in on came down the mountain valley, made a sharp right bank turn, and immediately touched down, with dust just boiling up behind it; it was a dirt runway. I asked Pete if we had done that approach yesterday – "Yep, you were asleep until we touched down." I said, "That looks a little dangerous," and Pete said, "It scared me." It wasn't but a few minutes later that a beautiful blue, twin engine plane came down the valley, made the same sharp turn, landed perfectly, and taxied right up to us. After the pilot hopped out and introduced himself, he said, "Let's load up; they have work for you; a friend of mine has a bad tooth;" so he strapped our small bags down, and asked me to hop in the co-pilot seat for a better view.

We were up and away over the beautiful Andes Mountains on a perfect morning for flying. I was amazed by the little foot paths and small homes at 16,000 feet, as we flew through a huge mountain gorge, and I asked if many people lived at that altitude. He said, "Some live at 18,000 in Peru, and they

3 – FUTURE PREPARATION

have huge lungs! Yes, we were in a different world. Soon we were gliding down over the Amazon basin, a huge jungle of winding tributaries. I asked, "What would happen if we were in a single engine plane and lost power?" "We would land on one of those little sandbars, and wait for a float plane." "Has that ever happened before?" "I don't think so, but the Helio Courier can land anywhere we have 200 feet to stop; it takes a little longer to take off, but we have never had an engine failure, because we have great mechanics." "You have mechanics where we are going?" "We are going to a little town in the middle of this jungle that has just about everything but a dentist." Then he asked me to enjoy the various trees as he flew lower, telling me, "There is nothing but snakes, crocodiles, piranha, and more snakes down in that swamp." Then he said, "Relax, the Lord will look after us" as he climbed up to a safer altitude. I heard him chuckling under his breath. In another half hour of raw beauty, we touched down at Yarinacocha (Yarina), an outpost for Wycliffe Bible Translators, better known in Peru as the Summer Institute of Linguistics (SIL), and Yarina was their primary field location in the middle of Peru – the middle of NOWHERE!

I could write a book about my experiences there, so I'll just touch on several of the highlights over 4 days in this little outpost. The printing press was right by the airport, and we could hear it clicking away, so we went in for a quick look where God was doing His work – a Bible translation is someone's "heart language," they said. Suddenly, the press just stopped, and they did not try to fix it; they prayed for the Lord to take over, and it started running again. I thought, "Wow, these are a different kind of people." They must have known what I was thinking, because one of them looked right at me and said, "This happens frequently, and prayer is the best cure." That had an indelible impact on me, and now in 2016, at this writing, I

Miracles Can Be Yours

pray when we have a malfunctioning piece of equipment at a critical moment in the office; most often, it works! I also pray silently when I can't find a little calcified root canal, and most of the time, my little file slides right into it!

So, back to Yarina; we were off in a little golf cart to the dental clinic where a couple of patients were waiting; one had a swollen cheek and an important canine tooth was sore to tap on – I see that every month in Rock Hill. Penicillin from the medical facility was not helping, and he wanted the tooth pulled. I told the patient that he would need root canal treatment to save the tooth. "Can you do a root canal?" I told him that I was a root canal specialist – well, he threw up his hands and said, "PRAISE GOD, I need a root canal, and WHO does God send, a specialist!" The clinic was fully equipped, with a real nice dental chair, high- and slow-speed drills, essential materials, and a good X-ray machine; however, it had NO WATER, so no suction! A construction team had just replaced the water line to the adjoining medical facility a few days previously and somehow had blocked off the line to the dental clinic. Fortunately, they were still there, and started to work right away restoring water for us – it took a few hours. I had given the man in pain some medicine I had with me, while we went to the house that had a room for us, and we had some lunch. Not thinking, I wet my toothbrush with the sink water, not the bottled water, when brushing my teeth afterwards!

We went back to the dental clinic and took an X-ray on our rejoicing patient. He had some minor decay that had infected the nerve (pulp) in his upper canine, with a LONG root. That would have been really tough to extract, but he was willing to have one of the plumbers at Yarina try to remove it. Yes, the previous dentist (over 2 years ago) had instructed two plumbers how to remove a tooth with IV sedation from the

3 – FUTURE PREPARATION

medical facility! It would still have hurt like the dickens without local anesthetic, and they had NONE. Furthermore, they would have probably broken the tooth off trying to get it out. Somehow, they heard about a dentist in Huánuco who might be willing to come – amazing how the Lord communicates! So with the suction working, I opened the tooth with no anesthetic, as the nerve was dead, and we got immediate drainage and pain relief. After a couple of minutes of suction he could tap on the tooth with no discomfort, and I completed the root canal treatment the next day – they had everything I needed, even long files! Unfortunately, I had to make multiple trips to the toilet much of that day – remember my tooth brush that I wet the day before? Well, it did not take but a few hours for the rumbling to start, and fortunately the medical clinic had some Flagel to nip my amoebic dysentery in the bud. I would have been down for a few days without it – "Thank you, Lord" was a common praise at Yarina.

When word spread about the painless root canal, I had several patients the next day, and I was able to find some *out of date* anesthetic tucked away in a cabinet, which *did* work, for an extraction and a few fillings. The medical facility had a new unmarried doctor, right out of medical school, who wanted to be a missionary doctor, so where better to experience his residency training than *in the field*? We shared some good conversation, and he showed me the swimming hole in the river that was netted off so the piranha could not intrude – that was nice! We took a dip, and the cool water really helped my tummy feel better, too. That evening, Uncle Cam Townsend, the founder of Wycliffe, happened to be on site, and he and his wife had Pete and me over for dinner; his house was very modest compared with other ones at Yarina. After dinner, he asked if I would like to listen to a recorded message from one of his favorite pastors in his study. I think he knew right where

Miracles Can Be Yours

I was spiritually, and sure enough, "The Battle for the Mind" from Charles Swindoll just nailed me to the wall, as it was just me and the Lord in that little study. Mr. Townsend then came in and prayed with me; I'll never forget that evening.

The most amazing thing for just about everyone at Yarina happened rather quickly! I was in bed early that evening after our visit with the Townsends, and heard some strange noises. I asked the man in the bunk below me, "Is that thunder?" He calmly said, "No, those are drum sounds; they occasionally send messages down the river at night when the birds get quiet." Then he said, "I think someone needs help." Sure enough, early the next morning, a float plane took off, and the medical clinic got a radio message that they were bringing in a very sick young man. Lots of people were waiting at the dock when the plane arrived, and I could see several men carrying a young man who appeared to be unconscious. His tribe many miles up the river worshiped boa constrictors, and the tribal leader thought the man was full of demons, so he was getting permission from the tribe that worshiped piranha downstream to throw him in the river. Well, that tribe had heard that there was a real doctor, the young physician, at Yarina, and told them to wait, then messaged Yarina for help. Yes, we were in a primitive place, but they did understand the principle of authority and permission.

Three men carried the young, unconscious man to the medical clinic, and the doctor started an IV with a penicillin drip, and I helped him undress the skinny frame of a man whom we estimated to be in his early 20s; he had large boils around his lower stomach area and his right hip. I lanced the one on his hip while the doctor opened the ones on his abdomen, and they drained immediately. The young man never moved. After a few minutes the drainage slowed, so we cleaned and bandaged the wounds, and I said, "I've seen a lot

3 – Future Preparation

of bad abscesses and cellulitis before, but nothing like this," and he had not either. He was hoping that it was staph infection rather than a ruptured appendix that had put him into toxic shock, and then he said, "I hope he makes it." We moved him to a room with a bed, checked on him throughout the day, and took turns changing his bandages every few hours, as they were still draining.

The young man did not regain consciousness at any time that day, and I could tell that Yarina's young doctor was very concerned when he went home. I was in the room that evening when an elderly missionary couple walked into the room, knelt down by the bed, and prayed a little prayer that I will never forget: "Heavenly Father, we come in the name of Jesus to ask that you would touch this man with the healing power of your Holy Spirit, and use him for your glory. We thank you for what you are going to do," and they said good evening to me, and walked out of the room. I went by to tell the physician about the couple, and he said, "They are great prayer warriors; I hope they are not disappointed in the morning; his vital signs are not good." I asked if I could go with him in the morning, and he said, "I'll meet you there at 6 o'clock." We had a little prayer together, and I went back to the home where we were staying for the night. Yarina's sunrise every morning, 365 days a year, is a little before 6:00 AM, and it gets light immediately, as they are close to the equator, and they have daylight 12 hours per day!

We heard some chanting noises as we approached the young man's room, and when we opened the door, he was out of the bed, standing by the window, had pulled out his IV, and his bandages were on the floor. He was afraid, so the doctor summoned a native Peruvian technician who could hopefully communicate with him; he did, and we were able to examine the young man. There was no sign of the incisions we had made, and THAT is a medical impossibility – yes, it was a miracle. I found out months later from John Bush that God had answered the missionaries' prayer completely; the man was nourished back to complete health, received salvation, and went back to his village, where he was instrumental in leading the village to Christ, and there was a little cross on their meeting room, rather than a snake. That is how God works in primitive areas!

The flight back to Huánuco was questionable that same day because of cloud cover over that area, and we postponed it for several hours. The word was, "We may have to fly directly to Lima the next day," as our flight to the US was the next afternoon. Finally, the word came from Huánuco – partial clearing! The *Evangel*, that beautiful little twin engine bird, was fired up, and we were off on a beautiful day at Yarinacocha; I left part of my heart there, and had a tearful departure as I hugged the doctor. We hit clouds at the base of the Andes and climbed to 21,000 feet, as the mountains around Huánuco peaked out at 20,000. So we were flying around above the clouds where the pilot thought Huánuco MIGHT be, and I was getting light headed due to the altitude.

Peru had a VOR (variable omnidirectional range) navigation station in Lima, but not one near Huánuco, so our pilot could not vector in; we just kept flying in circles. Our pilot put an oxygen mask on, and asked, "Are you OK?" We gave him thumbs up, but we were breathing heavily. Then he said, "If we don't find a hole in these clouds soon, we'll have to turn back." I was thinking, "Lord, please help us" when our pilot said, "There it is," and he tipped that little bird into a vertical descent! My stomach was in my back as we dropped several thousand feet in just a short time; it was a terrifying experience, and I almost got sick. He pulled out of the dive, made a few descending circles around the airport, mountains all around, and

3 – FUTURE PREPARATION

then leveled out with a perfect touch down! What a pilot! Pete and I were trembling as we shook his hand and took our bags. I can't even remember if he came to the construction project with us or stayed with the plane. Adrenalin was in my system for hours, and I had trouble sleeping that night, just reliving the whole experience in my mind.

We left the next morning with my mind still spinning with a big WOW, as I thought, "I go on a construction project, but God pulls me off site and does His own work; He was building faith and courage into my very being." Years later I understood that He was just getting me ready for more faith-packed adventures. After all, He knows the end before it even happens! He is GOD.

P.S.: The Bible translations are now complete in that area, and Yarina has been closed.

Chapter 4
Sudden Calamity

Home sweet home with Pam and bundle of joy, and it was not long before I was invited to share my story with several churches through various patients; I was surprised to discover that most churches in our area did not put much emphasis on the foreign mission field. With the need for *pain relief in primitive areas* seared into my very being, my faith strengthened, and my courage boosted to a higher level, I began to research where I might be needed with Wycliffe as a dentist. I had developed a deep respect for Wycliffe Bible Translators through the two Peru exposure trips, and I knew that their focus was on translating the Bible in people's own language.

Yes, Wycliffe had a multidenominational openness with no bickering about doctrine or superfluous denominational matters of manmade religion. They kept their eyes on Jesus and His Great Commission; I found churches that did not even know what the Great Commission was – how sad! One of the Wycliffe missionaries on furlough from the Philippines, living at the JAARS Center in Waxhaw, NC, had me over one evening for dinner. He was a pilot with JAARS (Jungle Aviation and Radio Service), and he and his wife *listened to me*, which is a lost art these days. Then they said, "God may use you more effectively by supporting other missionaries, rather than

4 – SUDDEN CALAMITY

being one yourself," and they prayed with me – another lost art. So as I prayed about it, and waited for the Lord's answer, it was confirmed by my pastor and other people I respected that short-term involvement for me, along with monthly financial support for needy missionaries already *in the field* may be a good fit for my family. Pam had grown up in Rock Hill, SC, and she was not excited about moving to a foreign country, away from her close-knit family. Furthermore, we were thinking about another child, and I was the only endodontist in a three-county area with over fifty referring dentists. Yes, the word from the Lord was clear: "Stay in Rock Hill."

Then when Pete, who was a great master of ceremonies for the Wycliffe banquet fundraising dinners in the Southeast US, suggested another translation center project in Peru, I was *on go right away*. The center in Huánuco was complete, and another one close to Huaraz, higher up into the Andes, needed some finishing touches. I thought, "I wonder if the same coordinator from the Huánuco project would be there needing a floor tile man," and verbalized that to Pete; we had a good laugh.

These translation centers were actually apartment complexes where families from the nearby villages would live, and their conversations would be recorded; then the recordings would be analyzed linguistically by computer. As I understood it – probably much more complicated than my understanding – the computer would then develop a phonetic alphabet to fit that particular language, and the translation of the New Testament could begin. Prior to this computer involvement, it would take 20 or 30 years of hard work by missionaries living within the various tribal villages to complete a translation; can you imagine the commitment that would take?! And I was giving up just 1 week of comfortable living, thinking that was a good sacrifice. Little did I know that "obedience is more important than sacrifice" (1 Samuel 15:22).

Miracles Can Be Yours

Pete and I recruited another friend of ours, Rick, to join us on the trip, so we were a threesome this time headed to South America. Huaraz had no airport at that time, so it was on the bus again for an adventurous trip. At one point on a mountain pass, we stopped to get a soft drink, and after just a few steps down the aisle of the bus, we were out of breath – it was 16,000 feet! The bus driver had fun watching us, and then getting our luggage from under the bus and walking away was a respiratory struggle. They had some special herbal tea ready to help us acclimate to the 10,000+-foot altitude at our project. Rick said the next morning, "I rolled over in bed last night, and was out of breath." Yes, the first couple of days working were tough, but they had me painting while I acclimated to the altitude. As I remember, I extracted a couple of teeth because I had some basic anesthetic and extraction forceps in my bag. I think Rick was using his computer expertise there at the center. Before we knew it, the final day of our trip was upon us, which meant an interesting side trip; this was a hallmark of the Wycliffe short-term trips.

Earthquakes are common along the coastal fault line of South America, and we were on the short trip to the ruins of the original city of Huaraz, which they said had been *devastated* by an earthquake in 1970 – *demolished* would have been a more appropriate word. Yes, an entire city of 16,000 people was a huge flat field of dried mud, with crosses sticking up everywhere homes were estimated to have been. I believe 25,000 had been killed in the surrounding area, and it all happened in an instant! The only part of the city that was visible was a small hill of a cemetery with little beehive-type tombs all around it. On the top of the cemetery was a 30-foot-tall statue of Jesus, with arms raised toward a huge 22,000-foot mountain towering over the city.

The Andes Mountains, which are truly majestic, make our beautiful Rockies look like the Appalachians, and as we stood

4 – SUDDEN CALAMITY

by the cemetery in awe of this huge mountain, our guide told us what had happened. The normal avalanches that came down from the mountain in previous years went through a large canyon which protected the city; however, during the earthquake of 1970, a large portion of the mountain broke off, resulting in a massive avalanche of mud that jumped over the canyon and instantly covered most of the city. It was about noon when this catastrophic event took place, and some of the home locations close to the remaining cemetery were excavated; they found people in their crushed homes with food in their mouths. Can you imagine having lunch with your family, and WHAM, tons of mud crushing you, without any warning?

The miracle of this tragedy was that not long before that earthquake, a supernatural revival had moved across the city, resulting in most of the residents receiving Christ as their Savior; hence, the large statue of Jesus being built on top of the cemetery – how ironic that the arms of Jesus were lifted toward the mountain. Lots of people in Peru, which was predominantly Catholic at the time, were really upset about this catastrophe, but many of the true Christians were using this as an evangelistic opportunity and a warning. Scripture is very clear when it says, "You shall suddenly be broken, and that without remedy" (Proverbs 6:15 and 29:1). Time and time again throughout history we have seen God's judgment coming quickly, and these events are just a mere glimpse of what will take place during the Day of the Lord; that will be a cataclysmic event that will collapse the entire universe!

Pete, Rick, and I came home with a whole new respect for the word *calamity*, with a vivid picture of the beautiful statue of Jesus permanently etched into our memory banks, His hands raised in authority as the King of Kings and the Lord of Lords. We were praising God for the truth of His Word, the commitment of Wycliffe Bible Translators to reach EV-

Miracles Can Be Yours

ERY language group, and for His protective hands over our bus ride back to Lima, which could have been another catastrophe for the lost people on that bus. How those roads are maintained in safe conditions with numerous rock slides every few miles was a mystery to us; yes, that was the last time Rick and I would put our faith to the test in a bus on those crazy mountain roads of Peru. The Lord knew that Rick and I in future years would desire to go to Machu Picchu, and He provided a train!

Chapter 5
Small Words – Big Impact

IF is a powerful little word, and I often tell people, "IF you are not having problems, then you are probably not an enemy of the Devil." On the opposite end of the spectrum, which goes hand in hand with the above, is a statement from now-deceased James Kennedy: "IF you are not interested in taking people to heaven with you, that probably means you are not going yourself." Small words like IF, BUT, and SO can be very powerful, as small does not necessarily mean insignificant. These conditional words are perhaps the ones we struggle with the most when it comes to life application, and are often the difference between doctrinal head knowledge and true heart faith.

So Rick and I were home sweet home again after our Huaraz encounter with a vivid picture in our mind's eye of *mass destruction etched into our memory banks*. Fortunately, *an awesome picture of Jesus* is on permanent record there, too. Pam and I were enjoying life and work in little old Rock Hill, when the dreaded word came from her doctor, "*Cancer*;" there is a *possible* in front of it, BUT the excruciatingly fearful *C word* is there. Yes, the possibility of cervical cancer is part of our life, so an immediate surgical procedure at Presbyterian Hospital was scheduled, and our minds were running wild! What if it IS cancer? What

Miracles Can Be Yours

are they going to do? Can we have any more children? What if it is metastatic? FEAR, False Evidence Appearing Real, is one of Satan's primary tools when attacking people, and he was pouring fear into our minds as we drove to the hospital. I gave my beautiful wife a kiss, to reassure her that all would be OK.

God showed up in a powerful way as I was sitting in the waiting room, and it was so amazing that I shall never forget the encounter. Pam was back in the operating area, and I was reading Psalms, sitting in the middle of a comfortable couch by myself; the waiting area was fairly quiet with 15 or so people there, some in quiet conversation. Soft music was playing, so I just closed my eyes and started praying silently with my Bible on my lap. After a few minutes, I felt each side of the couch beside me depress slightly, and then chills came all over me as I heard two distinct voices singing, "Jesus is the rock, He's the rock on which I stand" in a continuous chant, and it got louder and louder. The waiting room became overwhelmingly quiet, as the sweet sound of young girls' voices became very obvious. "Jesus is the rock, He's the rock on which I stand" kept me mesmerized; I kept my eyes closed, as I was almost afraid, with the presence of the Lord so evident around me.

After what seemed like several minutes, I felt a tap on my shoulder, and to my surprise, a nurse was there asking me to come with her. As I arose and looked around, I saw two precious little girls about 10-12 years old just singing their little message, and they continued as I left the waiting room. I asked the nurse as we walked down the hall, "Who are those little girls?" Her reply shocked me: "No one knows." I was dumbfounded for the remainder of our short walk, and the nurse ushered me into a small conference room, and said, "The doctor will be with you in a few minutes," and she walked out. I was still overwhelmed with the sweet spirit of the waiting

5 – SMALL WORDS – BIG IMPACT

room and I was supernaturally comforted by the fact, "Jesus IS my rock," when a doctor came in, shook my hand, and said, "We did a cone biopsy of her cervix, and the frozen specimen came back with all the borders clear." I thanked him and immediately told him about the waiting room experience, and he nonchalantly said, "Yes, we think they are angels." "Have you ever seen them?" I asked. "No, they just seem to come and go" was his response. "Come on, let's go meet them," I said with excitement. Little did I know then that God's messengers are on His schedule, not *our* desired time plan.

As we left the room and proceeded down the hall with haste, the doctor calmly said, "In case of any complication, we'll keep Pam overnight." As I opened the door to the main waiting room, I pointed to the empty couch where I was sitting, and the doctor kindly said, "Maybe I'll see them one day," as he gave me a little paper, saying, "Pam will be in this room # by the time you get there – you two take it easy – nice meeting you." I thanked him again for his expertise as he walked away, and thought, "Take it easy after I've had an angelic visitation!" I was overjoyed as I told Pam about the experience while waiting, and she was excited, too. Then I told her what the doctor said, and all of the human fear that we felt on the way to the hospital was long gone, replaced with Joy and Praise for what the Lord had done.

Yes, a great Christian doctor and a few guardian angels are all we need when our bodies get into disarray, but (there is that little word again) even when the report turns out to have negative consequences, we should STILL give the Lord praise, as our tribulations are, in reality, just momentary. After all, He IS the sovereign LORD of this universe, knowing even when a sparrow falls. However, we do live in a fallen world with numerous forms of invisible bacteria, viruses, fungi, molds, and various toxins entering our bodies every day, not to mention

Miracles Can Be Yours

the spiritual attacks of one third of the angelic hosts that were cast to this earth years ago, that are coming against us. So it is truly a miracle that we are healthy most of the time.

Fortunately, we have TWO thirds of the heavenly hosts on our side, and they can produce an invisible cloud of defense, along with the most powerful force in the universe – the blood of Christ – as a protective covering for sin. The question is, "How often do we put our armor on?" And if faith comes by hearing, "Why don't we read our Bible OUTLOUD every day?" The Devil does not know what we think; only God knows that, BUT the Devil does know what we say! And, the power of life and death does lie in the tongue, so I ask us all, "Are we speaking life or death?" How I got off on that little excursion I don't know; perhaps it is the Holy Spirit! Most people of the worldly mindset would probably call my excursions bunny trails of ADD (Attention Deficit Disorder), but I have found that when one learns how to cope through his distractions without medication, he develops the ability to Hyper Focus. When I'm in the middle of a root canal procedure, I don't even hear the phone ring! Perhaps we should call ADD that is under control HFA (Hyper Focus Ability)!

So, back to focus; we do have a host of agents against us, but (there is that little word again) we also have a little word called SIN, and we tend to rationalize that curse with an *IF* or a *BUT* all too often. I like what my pastor says: "We can choose our sin, but we can't choose the consequences." Furthermore, we are plagued by various types of sin as well: outright rebellious sin, presumptuous sin, sins of omission, and, perhaps the hardest to repent of, stronghold sins, which can be passed from one generation to the next. I know that personally for me, the sin of stealing (kleptomania) was passed down to me by my dad, and perhaps my grandfather before him, as an out-

5 – SMALL WORDS – BIG IMPACT

right plague to my brother and me, and it was only confession and the power of Christ that enabled us to repent. Yes, we were still tempted to steal out of habit, but we could finally say "NO" (another powerful, short word) to that demonic stronghold, as we prayed together one night years ago. We were arm in arm on a mountain top rock watching several 4th of July fireworks displays over two cities below, asking the Lord to set us free. Furthermore, that stronghold has been blocked by the power of Christ for both of my sons. They have never even switched a price tag, and I had mastered that little art as a teenager, 55 years before this writing.

So, what happened back in the hospital on that eventful day of my FIRST angelic visitation, before the Holy Spirit took me on an important side story? This is my FIRST book writing, and little excursions may take place on occasion; that may make the process less boring for everyone concerned – I hope so! Yes, I was *on fire* with the whole experience in the hospital, so much so that I had to share it with several of the patients near Pam's room. As she snoozed off and on, with the peace of God on her mind, I went down the hall, introducing myself to total strangers, asking for permission to share my angelic encounter in the waiting room. No one refused to hear my story, and I prayed with several patients, leaving them with smiles on their faces as they would say, "Thank you." Often the television would be turned off, as I sang the little truth, "Jesus is the rock, He's the rock on which I stand."

So, what is the moral of this little chapter? *IF* we would just be bold enough to share our spiritual highlights and blessings with others, they would be blessed, too, *but* we are often just *too* busy, and no one receives the real blessing the Lord intended. Yes, we are all "set free by the power of our testimony and the blood of the Lamb," (Revelation 12:11) so the question is, "Are you a willing participant in the Lord's KINGDOM busi-

Miracles Can Be Yours

ness?" As an evangelist friend of mine used to ask, "When was the last time you had the privilege of leading someone to the Lord?" There was usually silence in the room. Then he would ask, "When was the last time you tried?" Yes, indeed, *IF* we would be faithful in the little things, God will take care of the big things (Luke 16:10). He always has and He always will, *SO* (another small, conditional word) our blessings depend on our actions, or perhaps I should say, our obedience! Yes, Jesus says very clearly, "If you love me, you will obey me" (John 14:15). See you in Chapter 6!

CHAPTER 6
DIVINE APPOINTMENTS

Let's move from the short but meaningful words of Chapter 5 to some longer words like *hyperinflation*! In 1985, as Rick and I were riding from the airport into downtown Lima, Peru, I noticed a large billboard in Spanish with a big **265%** in the middle. I asked the taxi driver what that was all about, and he said, "That is our money market rate." Rick said, "What a money market rate!" The driver said, "Yes, but our inflation is over 300% now." Rick and his brother had their own computer business, and Rick was a master in banking software, so he was astonished. The following day, I changed some dollars to the Peruvian currency, and Rick asked, "What did you do that for? We are not shopping for 5 days." I asked him what he meant, and he just said, "Do the math;" then he explained to me that 300% inflation was like buying a hamburger for a dollar, and then 3 months later it would be TWO dollars. Peru had changed their currency to *Inti* that year and ONE *Inti* was worth ONE THOUSAND *Sole*, their previous currency the year before. It had gotten to the point that one needed almost a pocketful of money to go out to dinner. That was my first exposure to hyperinflation, which is actually more destructive than a depression.

Miracles Can Be Yours

Two years later, when Rick and I went back, there were hundreds of begging *street kids* outside the airport upon the arrival of the big American jet, parts of the beautiful city of Lima were almost in ruins, wrecked cars on the streets, and no more beautiful flowers. The street kids lived in cardboard boxes, and it was so depressing that it was another 2 years before Rick and I went back in 1989. That visit was a major shock to us, because Peru's underground police force, the *Shining Light* was shooting the street kids upon sight, as they were not good for tourism, and our departure flight was delayed almost 2 hours by order of the *Shining Light*. Wow, they had the power to close an international airport! So Rick and I decided that would be our last trip to the once beautiful, safe city of Lima. Yes, hyperinflation can be a powerful, decimating force that we cannot even comprehend in the United States. Not yet!

So let's go back to 1985 when my good friend Rick was helping me do some renovation work at the Wycliffe House there in Lima. We had the opportunity to take a side trip to Cusco and Machu Picchu; the latter is actually part of the Incan ruins at about 8,000 feet in the Andes Mountains of Peru. It is a mystery as to how it was built, and even today no one knows why or how it was used. It is actually considered to be one of the wonders of the world. Yes, it was an exciting train ride down the hill from Cusco, which is actually at about 10,000 feet, as I remember. We had taken a commercial flight from Lima to Cusco, stayed in a little hotel, and then took the train to Machu Picchu the next day.

From the train station it was a short, zigzagging switchback van ride up the hill to these amazing Inca ruins. How they placed those huge rocks together so perfectly back in the 15th century is a total mystery to sophisticated builders of our modern era, and some consider the walls and rooms on top of that mountain to be a miracle, but the real miracle for Rick and

6 – DIVINE APPOINTMENTS

me was at the airport in Cusco on the way home. We got to the airport early and were waiting in the Faucet Airline boarding section, boarding passes in hand, with about 30 other people, right across from the Aero Peru boarding area. The Aero Peru plane landed and people were exiting the plane, but our plane had not yet arrived; there were only TWO airlines in Peru back then. Rick knew a little bit of Spanish so he went up to the front counter to find out what had happened to our flight, as it was supposed to land before the Aero Peru plane.

We had been patiently sitting in our boarding section, admiring a huge cross on a mountain on the other side of the runway, and reading our Bibles and praying together, when Rick left me there by myself. After several minutes, the Aero Peru flight was boarding, and a stranger in plain clothes walked up to me and said, "You and your friend need to get on your flight now." I told him that our tickets were for Faucet Air, but he was insistent, saying, "You need to board now." About that time Rick returned with the bad news that our Faucet flight had been cancelled. The man said, "Go now; get on your plane," pointing to Aero Peru, so we picked up our carry-on bags and walked over to the Aero Peru boarding gate, handing the lady our Faucet boarding passes. She picked up the phone, had a brief conversation with someone, and opened the door for us to go and board the plane. I looked back at the stranger and waved; he just pointed up to the sky. As we were walking to the plane, Rick asked, "Who was that man?" and I responded, "I don't know; maybe an angel."

When we got on the plane there were only TWO seats left, just an aisle apart, but we were ON the plane, so we were obviously overjoyed. Looking back on this event, we were convinced that God had sent one of his angels to direct us to the other airline. There was no way that this plain-clothed stranger who spoke perfect English could have known our situation, and how

Miracles Can Be Yours

important it was for us to get back to Lima THAT DAY. We felt sorry for the people we left waiting for Faucet Air as our plane taxied out; Rick had found out that our morning flight was the only one into Cusco that day. In fact, planes cannot leave there after 11 o'clock in the morning because of the runway altitude and temperature; one of those aeronautical mysteries regarding LIFT!

Yes, the Lord lifted us right out of a situation that may have cost us lots of time, not to mention a rebooking fee back to home sweet home. On our flight from Lima back to Miami, Rick and I were praising God for the miracle of Machu Picchu, as well as the miracle timing of the Lord's divine appointment with one of His angels. Little did I know that God was preparing the man right across the aisle from me for another type of divine appointment!

Our flight was nice and smooth and Rick decided to take a little nap, so I pulled out my Bible and was reading Proverbs. The man across the aisle said, "Excuse me, sir; I couldn't help but overhear your conversation; did you really have an encounter with an angel?" I said, "Yes, that is the second encounter I have had; the other one was in a hospital waiting room. Would you like to hear about that one?" He said, "Most certainly; I don't know that I believe in angels." So I briefly told him what had happened in the hospital waiting room with the two little girls singing, "Jesus is the rock, He's the rock on which I stand," which was so reassuring to me. With wide eyes the man looked at me very intently and said, "Do you believe in Jesus?" I said, "I not only believe in Him, but He is alive and well inside my very being." Can I tell you how Jesus saved me just a few years ago?" He hesitantly asked, "What did He save you from?"

About that time the Holy Spirit took command and I said, "From a life of anxiety, frustration, a major problem with stealing, a marijuana addiction, and a hounding fear about the

6 – DIVINE APPOINTMENTS

future." Then he asked, "How did He do that?" so I responded, "It is really quite simple; I just confessed my sins to Him and asked Him to come into my life and take charge. I didn't hear any bells ringing or see any flashing lights, but I sensed an overwhelming peace like I had never experienced before. I was amazed that the ever-present fear I'd felt was gone, and I knew that something really important had taken place in my life. I began to read the Bible much more frequently, and I was shocked to realize that I could actually understand its meaning. Before then I thought the only way to get to heaven was to be a preacher or missionary." He said, "I have been trying harder and harder to get close to God but it doesn't seem to be working for me." I told him, "I had been in that same place with extreme frustration when a friend told me you can't get close to God as long as you have a life full of sin; just confess your sins to Him and He will get close to you. So I followed his advice and said a simple little prayer, and my life changed dramatically."

I could see a light come on his face as he understood me, so I asked him, "Would you like to pray a simple prayer right now and ask Jesus to come into your life?" To my surprise, right there in the airplane, he said, "Yes, I would." So I reached inside my Bible cover, and gave him a little tract that had a prayer of salvation and a place for him to sign and date it. I said, "I'll leave you alone so you can be with the Lord; please let me know if I can help in any way." I saw him sign the little tract, and a few minutes later he asked if he could look at my Bible for a moment, so I said, "Sure, why don't you read the first chapter of John and let me know what you think about that?" and I flipped over to the book of John and passed it across the aisle.

I silently prayed for him a few moments and he said, "Sir, I did not know that Jesus was God." I said, "Welcome to the

Miracles Can Be Yours

Kingdom of Light; now you are on the most exciting adventure of your life. I would encourage you to find a good Bible-believing church that preaches and teaches Biblical principles and life application, and I promise you, if you seek the Lord first, He will take care of all the little details of your life. He may even send an angel one day with an important message while you are waiting. One of my favorite verses in the Bible is so simple; it merely says, *'Be still and know that I am God'* (Psalm 46:10)." He thanked me, and asked if he could read some more of my Bible. I said, "Certainly; we have about 3 more hours on this flight." I looked over from time to time and saw him reading intently, and knew in my spirit that he had begun the most exciting excursion of his life – the Word of God. Yes, he had entered into the realm of real eternal life. Have you?

As we were preparing to land, I took my Bible, and gave him one of my business cards, saying, "If you ever need a painless root canal, please give me a call." Several years later, I did receive a call from him, and he asked me if I remembered the man on the flight from Lima. I told him that I would never forget him, and we spoke for a few minutes. He was in Miami, visiting his sister, who used to give him a hard time about his Christianity. He had just led her to Christ with the same little tract that he had signed back in 1985, and my business card was still inside the tract. I had a short prayer with him, and told him that I would see him and his sister in the sky one day! Will you be there?

CHAPTER 7
AN AMAZING MAN

Having made a firm commitment to the Lord of at least one mission trip each year, I began going to Mexico with my home church through an organization called Mission to The World (MTW). Between the various annual trips to Peru, I discovered that there were about 35 organizations that utilized dentists, and then later found out that the number one physical pain in the world was abscessed teeth; however, very few dentists were actually available to help meet the need. The Christian Medical Association was trying to recruit dentists and eventually became the Christian Medical Dental Association, but they still had a shortage of dentists. This was an absolute tragedy, as I would find out in later years, how primitive people took care of their dental problems. Physicians were really not trained in proper anesthesia for the mouth, and they certainly weren't trained on how to extract teeth, so numerous primitive measures were used; but that is for a later chapter.

So in 1986, with a team of six men, I was on a flight to Mexico City, which is the largest populated city in the world, then a flight down to Acapulco, which is another jet set stopover for people with multiple homes. It was somewhat like Lima, Peru, with beautiful homes, gorgeous flower gardens, and clean streets. From Acapulco we drove for several hours

Miracles Can Be Yours

through numerous small towns, and then the road became a dusty, narrow road to our destination. MTW had placed a medical missionary from Sweden in this little town that had a 30-bed hospital but no doctor! As we drove through the little town that had literally shacks for houses, there was the odor of open sewage in the streets, and I thought, "Who in the world would want to live here?" The hospital actually had a dental chair in a small room, but everything was covered with dust, and the entire hospital looked like it was 50 years old. Dr. Thomas who was a pulmonary specialist could have named his price anywhere in the world after he had done his research on tuberculosis (TB), so I wondered, "Why is he here?" God knows exactly what we wonder about, and He had an amazing answer for me my second night there.

I got to work right away cleaning up their small dental operatory and trying to get it arranged so we could see patients. To my surprise, a skinny, young-looking man walked in and said, "Hi, I'm To-mas," as he extended his hand to me. We shook hands and I said, "Dr. Fuller here; are you Dr. Thomas?" With a sweet smile on his face, he said, "Yes, but everyone here prefers to call me To-mas." I knew in my spirit right away that To-mas was actually HIS preference, and that was my first lesson in real humility, a pulmonary specialist who prefers to be called To-mas! He was very apologetic about the condition of the dental room, and asked if I would like to see the rest of the hospital.

As he gave me a tour of the little hospital, I noticed that it was immaculately clean, and he asked if I would slip little covers over my shoes when we went into the surgical ward. He was wearing thin white clothes and had sandals on his feet which he covered. I asked him if these were head net covers, and he smiled and gently said, "Yes; these are not as expensive as shoe covers." Little did I know then that he was like Jesus who had

7 – An Amazing Man

come to this poor little town to minister healing and love, but it was quite obvious as the week went by that everyone had tremendous respect for him, and loved him with great affection. Our team leader had previously explained to me that he had been there several years by himself, and had requested MTW to send a dentist, if possible, along with our construction team. Obviously, MTW had not passed the word to him that I was with the team because, as we finished our little tour of the hospital, he said, "Please forgive me, I did not know you were coming, so please take a siesta after lunch today and I will have your dental operatory nice and clean for tomorrow morning." I immediately thought, "Wow, this man is asking for forgiveness for someone else's incompetence." I would have put the blame on MTW for not letting me know, but God was teaching me an important lesson in respect for authority. Dr. Thomas would have never said anything unkind about anyone, and I am still, in 2016, trying to learn that lesson.

We had a wonderful lunch that day with Dr. Thomas and his hospital staff. Mexico's big meal is always midday with a little siesta afterwards. During lunch we met one of the cooks whose name was Daniel, and he was full of funnies. I will never forget his first instruction: "Don't drink our water because you will feel de tummy rumble, as our amoeba have fun; you must drink two cool beers, and then eat de little pebbles on the ground, and our amoeba will get drunk on de beer, and have a rock fight and kill each other." Dr. Thomas was cracking up with a wonderful, shaking laugh as he said, "Daniel has several medical warnings for you." Sure enough, he had a warning about the hot peppers, and how they were bad for numerous reasons. We had a great time of laughter before our siesta.

That evening we had primarily different types of fruit for dinner, and it was early to bed, as the sun went down about 7 o'clock, and our area generator was turned off shortly thereaf-

Miracles Can Be Yours

ter. The next morning, I took my dental suitcase with all of my supplies over to the hospital and the room was spotless. There were several people already in line for tooth extraction, as Dr. Thomas had put the word out just the day before that we had a dentist at the hospital, so I arranged my anesthetic and extraction instruments on a nearby table and saw my first patient in Mexico. As the day went on, word spread about painless extractions, and the waiting line got longer and longer; therefore, I began to anesthetize several patients at a time, and had them wait outside for profound anesthesia. I think some dentists don't wait long enough for good anesthesia before they begin their work, and perhaps that is why there is such a tremendous fear about going to the dentist.

I saw over fifty patients that day, and Dr. Thomas told me he had heard some good reports from my patients, and asked me, "How did it go for you?" I told him my only frustration was not being able to communicate effectively with the people, as I was not very fluent in Spanish. He invited me to his home for dinner that night, and said he would help me with my communication skills. I told him I didn't think I could learn as fast as he, but I would be willing to try. I had previously heard from our coordinator that he spoke nine languages fluently, and could read ten. His final words were, "Get cleaned up, and be there by 6 o'clock, so I can show you something exciting," and he drew out a little map for me, saying, "Don't turn here."

I told my team that I was going to Dr. Thomas's home for dinner, and that he wanted to show me something exciting, so I hopped into a quick shower, and had no problem finding his house before 6 o'clock, on a half-mile, extensively worn foot path that he walked four times every day. Yes, he went home each day for lunch and a siesta, but then back to the hospital for his rounds with patients.

7 – An Amazing Man

He had designed his house by himself, and had just three other skilled carpenters help him build it. Almost hidden, it was tucked into a hillside for cool bedrooms, very modest but unique. A fresh water spring in the hill ran through his kitchen and bathroom, and he had a homemade solar-powered generator for electricity. There was very little electricity for houses in that area of town, and I heard a few gasoline-powered generators running, but he did not like those – too much noise! Dr. Thomas had converted the hospital generator over to solar power for daytime use, and was working on galvanic current for night use. As he was telling me about that, his wife came in with their three young children; she was as gracious as he was, and all of them began preparing some fresh fruit, while we walked into his living room. He showed me his homemade radio station, through which he brought in the Gospel message each evening by shortwave out of Ecuador; his antenna was hidden in a tree up over his home. He told me that it was illegal to broadcast the Gospel in that area, so he had to conceal the antenna. He told me that it would not be long before he could receive the broadcast and asked if I would like to see that; I said, "That would be fascinating!"

Like clockwork, at 6 PM, he turned a few knobs on a little homemade box, and a light bulb that was soldered to a couple of coat hangers lit up. With a big smile on his face, he said, "It is going out 75 miles on AM radio right now; many people come to Christ through this broadcast." Then he said with all seriousness, "I have to be very careful whom I tell about this." I asked him what would happen if that information fell into the wrong hands, and he said, "They would probably burn my house down." I was shocked, and as he saw the look on my face, he said, "The Lord has protected me for 5 years here, and I don't think He is going to stop any time soon, but we live by faith." Then he said, "Now have a seat," pointing to a nice

Miracles Can Be Yours

chair that he had obviously made. "Let me help you with some Spanish for your patients tomorrow," and he rattled off a few short phrases, telling me what each one meant, and I thanked him, acting like I could retain all of that. He wanted to continue, but his wife saved me with, "You two come on in and have some fruit." I hopped right up and washed my hands in the free-flowing water of their kitchen sink, and we sat down with their children to a wonderful display of about eight different types of fruit. During the meal I asked Dr. Thomas how he wound up in Mexico, still wondering why he would like to live in such a poverty-stricken area with open sewage in places.

He told me that during his residency in Sweden he had heard about some unusual TB cases in this area, so that was his first trip to their little hospital where he met a beautiful nurse; and he looked over at his wife with a most adoring smile. "I was only here for 2 months, and during that time period she was the main person the Lord used to lead me to Christ," he said with a voice of gratitude. He added, "She gave me my first Bible before I went back to Sweden." Then he shared how he published his research, and had numerous offers from various hospitals, so he went to Germany for 6 months; but he said, "I was making lots of money, but I was miserable." He could not get the little hospital in Mexico out of his mind, so he came back, and proposed to that beautiful nurse; they were married and he built their modest house. At one point he thought they might move to the United States but he realized that this place was a paradise. I asked him, "Why would you think that?" I will never forget, with almost an angry look on his face, he said, "We have clean air here, and as a pulmonary specialist I can appreciate that, clean fresh water; we have trees that produce fresh fruit year round, we grow our vegetables right outside; the people here really love me, and they need me."

7 – An Amazing Man

I think he saw the shocked look on my face, as he continued, "Every year my wife and I borrow a friend's car for the 3-hour drive to Acapulco to celebrate our anniversary at the same hotel where we had our honeymoon." All I could say was, "Wow, that is an awesome story; you DO have a paradise right here." It was dark by the time I left, so he said, "I'll show you the way back," and got his little electrostatic flashlight that he had made, and off we went. He pointed out several nocturnal animals on the way, saying, "This place is amazing." We had a wonderful week together, but he never asked me if I would consider moving there; I think he knew what I would have said. He was brilliant in so many ways, and certainly blessed by the Lord with tremendous discernment. Perhaps that is the gift that comes with *complete obedience*.

Yes, beauty is definitely in the eye of the beholder, and "righteousness with contentment is a means of great gain" (1 Timothy 6:6). Here was a man who worked diligently 6 days a week, performed cesarean births for $2.00, yes, TWO U.S. dollars, as well as other abdominal surgeries for ONE dollar, did not own a car because he didn't need one, truly loved his family, and everyone in the community loved him; I guess that is as close to paradise as one can get this side of heaven! I showed him how to extract teeth my final day there, and left him my basic surgical elevators and extraction forceps. He was a most grateful man, because that was a real need in which he had no expertise; he hugged me several times and his wife was ecstatic. Amazingly, he knew just about everything about mechanics, electronics, and computer technology.

Our team leader was astounded by some of the questions he was asking about computers – questions he had never even thought about. At the church service before we left that amazing little town, the pastor asked in Spanish, "To-mas, Amazing Grace, please?" My good friend responded with the *page num-*

Miracles Can Be Yours

ber for Amazing Grace in their little hymnal; yes, he had a photographic memory as well, and had memorized all the hymns, including the page numbers. We all went home knowing we had been in the presence of a truly godly man, a brilliant one at that. I had a sore right hand from numerous extractions and the other members of our team were exhausted, but satisfied because they had completed ALL the work on the house.

MTW closed out that project, and to my knowledge, Dr. Thomas never requested help for anything else. I will never forget that phenomenal man, because he demonstrated to me what humility, gratitude, and contentment are all about. I wish every doctor in the United States could spend a week with him; we would have a much healthier country, and much more contented physicians. Finally, I went home AGAIN, with my pride on the back burner. I went there thinking, "I am a real servant, giving up a whole week of production." Years later I would realize an important truth, "There is one who has great riches, and yet has nothing; and there is one who makes himself poor, and yet has great riches" (Proverbs 13:7). Lord willing, I'll see you in Chapter 8.

Chapter 8
Up Close and Personal

Hello and welcome back; we never know when we are going to take our last breath, do we? Yes, there is a time to be born and a time to die, and on each end of that spectrum there can be ecstasy or tragedy. Personally, I cannot speak to the tragedy of death during childbirth, or, for that matter, the loss of a teenage child through a texting auto accident, and that senseless fatality will probably become more prevalent; they say that losing a child is the ultimate agony a parent can endure. However, I can speak to the transition of a parent becoming a dependent child again, the frustration of that, and then the parent's passing away.

As you may remember, I lost my dad to a very painful departure with cancer when I was a senior in college, and that was a 2-month painful excursion for my entire family, especially my mom. Nevertheless, I got to see all of their petty conflicts and antagonistic behavior toward each other turn to an outpouring of complete love before he passed away; yes, love may be late, but it never fails. My mother was from Scotland and a very stubborn Scott at that. Her maiden name was Cruden, and her father was in the lineage of the man who wrote *Cruden's Complete Concordance of the Bible*; some people say he went crazy doing it. I certainly hope that I don't regress to that stage preparing this book, my first and perhaps only! (That was supposed to be funny, so I hope I can hear you laughing.)

On a serious note, my mother used to say, "I am Anglican," and she was proud, proud, and more proud of that statement; however, she did not know the Lord. She used to tease me about going from marijuana to Jesus, just like my brother did, and both of them told me that one day I "would come around." Well, that day never came, and the Lord graciously used me to lead both of them to Christ. My mom and dad, as most of their generation, were both heavy smokers, unfiltered Camel cigarettes, in fact, and they both developed lung cancer. Unfortunately, my dad's was not caught in time before it metastasized to his brain, and it ultimately ravaged through his entire body. The first clinical manifestation of that disease was his inability to write, and then his speech went within days. The Navy Base Hospital in Charleston, SC thought he was suffering from a mild stroke, and recommended bed rest; well, so much for the treatment of a veteran. He was retired from 33 years of military service, and his discharge chest x-ray revealed a spot on his left lung, but it was noted as *probable artifact*. *If* they had only kept an eye on that, or let him know, he could have perhaps lived for many more years, but *if* is a very significant word, as we know.

Mom, on the other hand, was a little more concerned about her health after the passing of her husband, and her cancer was caught in early stages, and was treatable. After extensive radiation treatments, which were very detrimental to her quality of life, she became rather pessimistic about most things. I convinced her to sell the big house on the Ashley River in Charleston, and move to Greenville, where she had many sweet memories of our early family years together, and she would be closer to me in Rock Hill. She really enjoyed her little town house in Greenville; however, her health continued

8 – UP CLOSE AND PERSONAL

to decline even though she had five different doctors: her general physician, internal medicine specialist, cardiologist, and two oncologists. I became so frustrated, because they never seemed to agree on which medications she should be taking, or what dosage was best, but that is another story.

Yes, watching a parent become systematically debilitated can be a painful experience, especially when the parent doesn't know the Lord. Mom knew all about Jesus, but she certainly didn't know Him with any type of intimacy. She had her standard little Anglican prayer that she would say before meals: "For what we are about to receive, may the Lord make us truly thankful." But that was it; dead religion, "I am Anglican." And the crazy thing is, she had no desire to go to church!

Greenville was about an hour and a half drive from our home in Rock Hill, and I would try to go there at least every few weeks. I will never forget ONE evening when I went there, prepared to just listen to her talk for an hour, but the Holy Spirit had something else in mind. After listening to her negativity regarding numerous issues, (I was praying the whole time) somehow, the one-way conversation turned into joyous mutual memories about the old days in Greenville, with some laughter from both of us. The Holy Spirit prompted me to get down on my knees in front of her chair, and with tears in my eyes, I asked her if she could forgive me for some of the bad things I had done. She gently stroked my bald head and said, "Oh, Noel, you have been a wonderful son." I said, "No, Mom, I've done a lot of bad things, and some of them even toward you, like stealing; could you please forgive me?" Without hesitation, she said, in her best Scottish accent, "Why, of course I can."

I had not planned on sharing the Gospel with her that night, as in the past she would become a little irritated; however, at that moment, the Holy Spirit gave her a picture of forgiveness, and how quickly it can be issued. She said, "Maybe I need to ask God to forgive me for many of the things I've done." I said, "Well, Mom, would you like to ask Him right now?" When the Holy Spirit is in charge, everything just falls into place without one even thinking about what one needs to say, and that night, numerous verses of the Bible spontaneously came through my voice. My sweet mom, with joy and weeping, asked God to forgive her, gave her heart to Christ, asking Jesus to take charge of her life. We were both rather ecstatic, to say the least!

Our subsequent *tele talks*, as she put it, were mostly about what the Lord was doing; it was exciting! I think it was the next month when Pam, Sam, and I had been to Lake Jocassee, our favorite little getaway, not far from Greenville, that we stopped on the way home to see Mom. I suggested that she pray about moving into the nearby Dogwood Manor that I had contacted, or have someone come and live in her home with her, as she was physically getting weaker. I can hear her right now: "I am NOT going to an old folks' home, and I am NOT going to have someone live in my home with me." So again, I told her to pray about it, and God would make it clear to her what she needed to do. We had prayer with her, and she could not stop kissing her precious little grandson. He called her "GranGran," and she loved that.

Unfortunately, she never got to hear "GranGran" again, as just 2 days later, I received a call from the hospital saying that she had fallen and broken her arm, and was not doing very well. I spoke with her, and she said, "The Lord doesn't seem to be answering my prayer very well, does He?" and added a little laughter, as she so often did. I reassured her that I would be up that weekend for a nice visit. She said, "I hope so," and I knew she was depressed. Unfortunately, I needed to get to a patient, so I had to cut our conversation short.

8 – UP CLOSE AND PERSONAL

The next day, the hospital called and said that she had slipped into a coma, and things did not look good. I thought, "Oh, No," cancelled the afternoon patients, and was ready to leave, when the mailman arrived with his usual stack of mail. I almost did not go through it, but there was the little cassette tape that I received monthly from the Maranatha Singers. For some reason, I opened it, and played it as I drove to Greenville; it gave me amazing comfort, and it was entitled *Psalms Alive*, by a group named Praise. I had a little cassette recorder in the back of the car, so I took the tape into the hospital with me. Mom was lying there with her eyes open, but there was no reaction to my hand over her face; yes, she was in a deep coma.

I knew that hearing was the last sense to go, and that quite often, people could hear while they were in a coma, so I spoke to her for a few minutes, and told her I was going to put some comforting music on. I started the tape and it played halfway through, so I turned it over and started the flip side. The entire time, I had been just sitting beside her bed reading my Bible and praying. To my amazement, I heard, "Noel, can you turn the music up?" It had always been "Turn the music down," but now she wanted it louder! She did not want to speak to me, even though her eyes could focus on me; she just wanted the music loud, and me to hold her hand. I played that tape about three times, louder and louder, and she, amazingly, came out of the coma, seemed alert, and started speaking to me. I was amazed; not a single complaint!

The music was so loud that the nurses came down from their station to see what was going on, so I turned the tape off, and they asked, "Mrs. Fuller, can we get you anything?" She laughed and said, "Chateaubriand for two with Cabernet Sauvignon, please," and we all laughed. She struggled a little with her breathing that night, so I called my brother who was about 5 hours away, and told him that he needed to come

Miracles Can Be Yours

down right away. Mom and I snoozed off and on that entire night, and quite often she would wake me up by saying, "Noel, can you put the music on?" and we played it fairly loud most of the night.

The next morning, the doctor came in early and he was shocked that she was conscious and able to talk. He told Mom that he was going to speak to me privately for just a few moments. WELL, Mom said without much hesitation, "Whatever you have to say, I want to hear it," in her stubborn Scottish accent. So the doctor said that obviously the tumor had metastasized to her neck, blocking the blood flow back to her heart, so her carotid veins were extremely distended, and then he said, "I don't know how you came out of the coma, but you did; we'll get you some more medicine so you can breathe easier and be more comfortable." Mom amazed me when she said, "Young man, are you a Christian man?" He said, "Well, I go to Saint Francis Church." Immediately, Mom jumped in, and said with her failing voice, "I was an Anglican all my life, and I'll tell you right now, Christianity has nothing to do with CHURCH; it's all about knowing Jesus," and she coughed a little. He backed up a few steps and patted Mom on the ankle, saying, "Now, Mrs. Fuller, you have a good day, okay?" Continuing to struggle with her breathing a little, Mom said, "Just remember, young man, it's all about Jesus; His angels are here right now, so I don't need any more medicine, please." Coughing a little, she asked, "Do you understand, young man?" He said, "Yes, ma'am; I'll leave you two alone," as he walked out of the room.

My mom had been through the terrible London bombing of World War II, and had seen more than one person's fair share of tragedy; she had even lost her brother, as his tank was blown up in North Africa, and they got a telegram to that effect, which had to be heart wrenching. And then she was by

8 – UP CLOSE AND PERSONAL

my dad's side constantly through his very painful state, overdosed on morphine, but he hung on to hope for over a week, when things were hopeless, so she was no novice to death. After the doctor left, I told her that Calvin was on the way down and asked her to hang on so he could see her. She kept asking me, "Can you hear those angels?" We had turned the tape recorder off when the doctor came in, and it was quiet in the room, but she kept saying, "I hear them singing; you don't hear that?" It was just a few minutes after that, with a smile on her pale face, she said, "Bye bye, Noel," and just stopped breathing. I checked her pulse, and it was gone! I felt agony and joy at the same time, knowing that she was with the Lord.

About that time, a nurse rushed in and said, "Is she OK? Her monitor stopped." I said, "Yes, she's fine now; she is with the Lord." The nurse told me right away that the most unusual thing had happened during the night; no one had requested any pain medicine, and she did not think that had ever happened before. Then she said, "Perhaps that praise music that we could hear at the nurses' station brought ministering angels into this wing last night." I asked her to please share that at their next staff meeting, and perhaps they could start having praise music played in the hospital and reminded her that God inhabits the praise of His people. Then she said, "Are you sure you are OK?" I told her that I was sad and happy at the same time – she understood with a big smile.

My brother Calvin arrived about an hour later, and was visibly upset that he had not seen Mom recently, and now she was gone. I told him the amazing story about her departure, and he thanked me. Then he said, "Maybe I'll have your faith one day," so I reminded him that faith comes by hearing, and that maybe he should start reading his Bible more, and asking God for saving faith. I think he actually received that, because it was several years later that he surprised me with a story

Miracles Can Be Yours

about answered prayer with his youth group. I said, "Why didn't you tell me that you know Jesus?" and he laughed and said, "I did not want to hear you preach to me again," and he gave me a big hug, saying, "Thanks, bro." That was another awesome day!

However, before that happened we had some major controversy over where Mom's money was going to go, which is not an uncommon occurrence after someone dies. Calvin had hired an attorney who was already making calls to my Aunt Sheila in London. Mom had changed her will, leaving everything to her sister, and Calvin was irate. "Dad would not have wanted that money to go to her," he said several times, and I had to keep reminding him that it was no longer Dad's money. I showed Cal in the Bible, "A brother offended is harder to win than a strong castle" (Proverbs 18:19), and he asked, "So why are you doing this?" I said, "Because Mom wanted it this way, simple as that." Then I showed him in Proverbs again, "Settle the contention with the lot" (Proverbs 18:18), and he said, "What the hell does that mean?" I told him, "Just what it says," as I handed him a quarter. "This isn't between you and me; it is between you and God; what do you want?" He wanted a certain amount of money for his sons' college education, so I said, "OK, you flip the coin, and if you win, it will go into a trust fund specifically for their education, and if they don't use it, the money goes to Aunt Sheila – agreed?" He agreed, flipped the coin, won the flip, picked up the phone, and called his attorney, leaving him the message, "Thanks, but I don't need you anymore." We hugged and his boys went to college several years later. I tell you that personal story, just to remind you that the Lord has the perfect way to settle contentions, and I have used that a few times in settling disputes between my sons, with no further conflict. By the way, the Fuller family now has FIVE generations of two boys, starting with my great

8 – UP CLOSE AND PERSONAL

grandfather through my two grandsons. Hopefully, we won't need any more coin flips!

Well, we've just been Up Close; let's get Personal, OK? If you are anything like me, you may not finish this book – sort of an ADD thing, I guess. So, why leave the most important conversation to the end of the book, right? You have heard a few stories about *Knowing the Lord*, and *Serving Him*, SO – where do you stand? Do you know, for certain, that when you die, or if Jesus comes before that appointment, that you will be with the Lord in Paradise? Please think about that; if He comes back before you die, will you FOR SURE be with Him in the clouds?

The simple, sovereign truth is as follows: Jesus IS the Son of God, who was sent to this earth as a virgin-born baby, lived an amazing, perfect life in constant communion with his Heavenly Father, willingly died for all who would receive Him as their Savior, descended to Hell to take the keys of death for His people who will serve Him, rose from the grave through the power of the Holy Spirit, was seen alive by hundreds of people, ascended into the clouds visibly before His disciples, and the most glorious thing is yet to come – He is coming back! All of this is clearly verified in the Bible, the most persecuted book of all times, and the best-selling book of all times; yes, the ONLY religious book to have the majority of its prophetic prophecy come true, letter perfect.

Noel Fuller cannot convince anyone regarding eternal life, but as my pastor says, "We can deliver the mail;" *The Holy Spirit is the only one who can convince*, so if you are a skeptic, please ask Him, the Holy Spirit, *to reveal to you your need for Jesus*, and then follow His prompting, no matter what the cost. Or if that is too complicated for you, just cry out to Jesus, *"Please save me."* I promise you, the more you become intimate with Christ, the more you will love him, and when you love him, the more you will willingly obey Him, out of gratitude for how much

Miracles Can Be Yours

He loves you, and what He did for you – the exchange of His righteousness for your sin on the cross. That gift cannot be assumed; it must be received by faith.

I encourage you, please don't try to stand before the Judgment Seat of Christ without Him as your cover – the consequences will be catastrophically painful and permanent if His blood is not covering your sin. Yes, "It is appointed, once for man to die, and then comes the judgment" (Hebrews 9:27). So, I give you plain and simple truth; your choice to receive it or reject it; I pray that I will see you in the sky one day. Just think, we'll all have perfect teeth!

Please take the time, right now, to finalize this matter, as *there may be a time when it is too late*. You certainly do not want God to laugh at your calamity (Proverb 1:26) – do you? Some people ask, "Why would a loving God send anyone to Hell?" For sure, He does not *SEND ANYONE*, but He does *ALLOW* people to go, which is a big difference! So once again, is your eternal destiny in heaven secure?

My Spiritual Birth Certificate

_____
DATE

_____
SIGNATURE

    Heavenly Father, please be merciful to me a sinner. I am sorry for my sins, and need your help for me to repent of my many sins. I believe that your son, Jesus Christ died for me, and that His precious blood will cleanse me from all my sin. By faith, I now receive Him into my heart as my Lord and Savior; trusting Him for the salvation of my soul. Help me Lord to do your will, and please make me into the person that YOU want me to be. I pray this in the powerful name of Jesus. Thank you Lord for what YOU are going to do in my life.

Chapter 9
Horsley Green

I have a good friend in Guyana, South America who says, "Your position determines your direction and your direction determines your destiny." I would certainly hope, if you are continuing to read this book, that you are a Christian, and this simple little statement about our position is actually very profound. Our position *in Christ* will definitely influence every path we take, IF we are obedient to the promptings of the Holy Spirit; and that certainly is a very big IF. The Lord definitely will allow us to get out of His will for a while, but in my experience, He has always led me back to the true path. However, I have known several people who have fallen completely out of His will, and actually become defiant and rebellious toward the Lord; they may have been what I call *churchians*, and not true Christians, but only the Lord is judge of that scenario. Hebrews 6 addresses that matter very precisely. So what does all of this have to do with our chapter title, Horsley Green? It has EVERYTHING to do with it! God will definitely direct our steps (Proverbs 20:24). If we obey Him!

I'm sure you remember the little dispute my brother and I had in the previous chapter regarding Mom's will; well, Horsley Green is about 35 miles from my Aunt Sheila's house in Hounslow, London, and it *just so happened* that Wycliffe Associ-

Miracles Can Be Yours

ates was having a construction project at Horsley Green at the very same time, June 1989, and I needed to get over to London to take care of probate matters with my Aunt. Now just how ironic is that?! Some people would probably think this to be just irony, but I happen to believe that *the Sovereign Lord of this universe was directing my steps very precisely, and I happened to be listening to Him.* Yes, my position in Christ was definitely directing my steps, and I have seen this time and time again. Sometimes from our perspective, it is hard to see God working in our present circumstances, but the Lord's sovereignty is present tense *all the time*, and we only realize and appreciate this when we look back and see how He was in charge of every detail, especially when He disciplined us.

Some people recommend that we keep our focus in the present, with a little emphasis toward the future, and they do not recommend looking back; however, I think looking back in a reflective and contemplative manner is very healthy, as well as giving us great insight into how the Lord has arranged our course. That is exactly what I am doing now, as I arrange my thoughts for these chapters, and it has been a major blessing for me, and, hopefully, for you, too. The apostle Paul does say, "Forgetting those things which are behind and reaching forward to those things which are ahead, I press toward the goal for the prize of the upward call of God in Christ Jesus" (Philippians 3:13), but I think he means to forget the things that distract our obedience and forward movement in Christ. I'm no theologian, but the Lord has given me some practical insight. Pam and I looked back on some family pictures a few weeks ago during our snow day, and it was WONDERFUL revisiting those sweet memories, and thanking the Lord for His providence. So, here's to going back!

I was off to London with my dental case of anesthesia, basic extraction instruments, and the same little tape player that

9 – HORSLEY GREEN

I took into the hospital the day before my sweet mom made her departure from this earth. I am convinced that if she had not heard that recording, she would not have come out of the coma, nor would we have had a wonderful final evening together. I think you know what I had in mind regarding my visit with Aunt Sheila, as it certainly was not removing a tooth. My previous visit to England came when my mom treated the two of us to a 1-week trip all around England as a college graduation present, so I had not seen my Aunt Sheila in almost 20 years. Her opening greeting was, "Oh my, what a grown man you are now!" I could tell that she was very uncomfortable when I started talking about how Mom had come to Christ, and just the mention of Jesus produced a frown on her face. Yes, my dear Aunt Sheila was Anglican, and she did not attend church, just like my mom.

We had a really nice walk in a garden close to her modest apartment and reminisced about our visit almost 20 years previously. She kept saying, "My, how you have changed." I was tempted to say, "Yes, I've been to Hell and back," but I knew better, so I mentioned the tape I had taken to the hospital, and how miraculous it was that Mom had come out of the coma through listening to the music. To my surprise, she was very receptive to that, and said in her Scottish accent, "My, my, music is certainly a wonderful thing, isn't it?" So I gave her the details of exactly what happened in the hospital that final evening with Mom, and the next morning with the doctor. She was rather speechless except for wanting to know more about Jesus's angels, and I explained to her that two-thirds of the hosts of heaven are on Jesus's side. She asked, "Where is the other one-third?" so I told her that they were on Lucifer's side in the kingdom of darkness. Her only comment was, "My, my!"

After a moment of silence, I asked her if she would like to hear that tape, and that I had brought the same little cassette recorder with me that I had taken into the hospital. She laughed and said, "You don't think I'm on the verge of death, do you?" with a big British laugh. I laughed along with her and said, "No, but we never know when we are going to take our last breath, do we?" There was more silence, so I said, "Let me show you how to work this little machine right now," and without hesitation, pulled it out of my carry-on bag. Surprisingly, she was very interested, so I showed her how to push the play button.

After a few minutes, she said, "My, my, it really is beautiful music, isn't it?" and we listened to the first few songs. I could tell she was somewhat uncomfortable without much conversation going, so I turned the tape player off, and showed her how to rewind the tape, eject, and flip it over when the first side was through. When I told her I was going to leave the recorder with her she said, "Oh, No, I would not think of that." I immediately responded, "You don't have to think about it; this is my gift to you, just like Heaven is a gift from Jesus." She looked me square in the eye and said, "Let's not get into that, YOUNG MAN; I will make you a cup of tea," and she got up and walked out of the room.

I knew right away that I had pushed the envelope of opportunity a little bit too far when she said "young man" with a firm voice, just like my mom used to do. I went into the kitchen, and we *chit chatted*, as the British say, a little bit while she boiled some water. The British are very particular about how they make their TEA, so I did not suggest that I help. It wasn't very long before her two sons and daughter came over, and they, too, were surprised how much I had changed since college graduation. I was tempted to tell them how the Lord had pulled me out of a pit, but I had exciting things on the agenda for this visit, and I really needed to leave for Horsley

9 – HORSLEY GREEN

Green within the hour. I asked them to please sit down because I had some important news from my sweet mom to share with them. They all reminded me in the typical stubborn British confrontational manner that the British say "Mum," and I reminded them that I was American, in my typical half-Scott bloodline.

Mom knew that Sheila had three children in 3 years, and that her husband had walked out on her, leaving Sheila with a hard life as a seamstress, living in a little apartment, and now she had three grandchildren to look after as well. Her oldest son was about 10 years younger than I, and had spent a good bit of his life in the pubs and racing cars; her second son and his wife were obviously not really happy, and her daughter had three children and was also divorced, so it had been tough for all of them.

Aunt Sheila had previously shared with me during our little chit chat time that several months ago, a rude man from the US had called her a few times with some personal questions, but she had flatly refused to answer any of them. "Why, the audacity of that man!" was her comment. However, she had no idea that my visit to bring her some amazing news about some money from Mom was related to that call. I said, "I'll be brief, because I really need to get over to Horsley Green. I have a little envelope for you, Aunt Sheila, from Mom; she wanted you to have a house." Immediately, she said, "Why, there is no way we could afford a house." I simply said, "Well, you can now," handing her the envelope. With a surprised look on her face, she opened the envelope, pulled out the check, and said, "Oh, my god, we can now," and threw everything into the air!

Needless to say, there were quite a few tears and hugs, and I left my sweet Aunt Sheila with some Biblical seed from the

Miracles Can Be Yours

Holy Spirit, and the compact tape recorder which she played so frequently over her final years. In her stubborn way, just like my mom, Aunt Sheila softened, and she, too, passed away with cancer, but not before coming to know Christ as her Savior. I had the privilege of stopping by London several times on my future trips to Kenya, even with Pam and our youngest son one time, about 10 years after this most important introduction to *saving faith* for my sweet Aunt Sheila. What a privilege to be the father of two sons, and even more of a privilege when the Lord directs our steps to serve as His *spiritual instrument* in the lives of other people, especially our family members!

At Horsley Green I used most of the anesthetic I had in my bag, helping several Brits who typically have *poor teeth*, as they say. I also became an expert at putting plaster on top of perfectly good sheet rock, but that is the way they do it! Being a handy helper with Wycliffe Associates meant doing the things *the way they ask, the way they do it*, whether it be mixing concrete in doughnut rounds on the ground in Mexico, laying floor tile in Peru, or plastering an entire wall of perfectly smooth sheet rock in England. It is a great test in simple obedience, and if we could only do that when it comes to spiritual matters, like obeying the Lord, *the way He asks, when He asks*, in the simple things! When we do the simple things, He will challenge us with more complex and important matters, as I discovered years later.

I have heard it said, "*Delayed obedience is disobedience,*" and that is more important than we realize. Also, our attitude is equally important; the Bible has much to say about cheerfulness. Yes, perhaps my favorite verses regarding His will are so simple: "Rejoice always, pray without ceasing, in everything give thanks" (1 Thessalonians 5:16-18); we would be much

9 – HORSLEY GREEN

happier and more contented people if we could just grasp the simplicity of that request. It is typical that most people think "Jesus wept" (John 11:35) is the shortest verse in the Bible, but I like "Rejoice always" (1 Thessalonians 5:16) because of its practical benefits. I'll see you in Chapter 10 in Jamaica with my family, a few years later.

Chapter 10
Family Evangelism Excursion

Five and a half years after the birth of our first son, the Lord provided for our second amazing son, on October 19, 1988. I watched with exhilaration as his tiny pointed head opened into a rounded full size head, and then one arm after the other proceeded out during birth. Then our doctor took Pam's hands, placing them around his chest, and said, "Pull from your womb this child which is *fearfully and wonderfully made*" (Psalm 139:14). I shall never forget Pam's face of *awe and love* when she looked at our trembling tiny baby. As the nurses were cleaning Mike, our doctor looked at me, asking, "Don't you have another son?" I said, "Yes, he is in Rock Hill with Pam's mom." Immediately, he responded, "Go get them, they need to be a part of this." One of our favorite family photos is of our 5-year-old holding the hand of his baby brother just hours after his birth. Yes, family is certainly a beautiful word, and one day, all Christians will fully comprehend *the glory of the family of God*, when we meet together in the clouds.

A good-looking young man by the name of Hank Williams came to Rock Hill in 1990, and asked me if I would be the Finance Director for an evangelistic crusade the Lord called him to bring to our community. We had a very nice visit and I think I asked him if he could sing; he told me that he actually

10 – FAMILY EVANGELISM EXCURSION

was named after the singer Hank Williams, but that he could not sing. I found out later that he actually had a fabulous voice, but I think all of us tend to minimize our gifts. Hank was also a pretty good natural athlete, and as we became friends, we had several rounds of golf together, and then participated in a basketball game in Russia. The latter was a resounding defeat for the United States evangelistic team, but that is another story!

Hank's greatest gift was his ability to communicate straight to the heart, and he had mastered the art of *delivering effective word pictures as he preached.* If you are assuming that I became the Finance Director for the Rock Hill crusade you are correct, and it was a wonderful experience for me getting to know the Hank Williams Evangelistic Ministries team. A major asset in that team was his beautiful wife Mary Ann, and they also had two young sons, so we had quite a bit in common, which really enhanced the close relationship that would develop between us.

I had come to the Lord through a confrontational, one-on-one approach to evangelism, and I often wondered about the effectiveness of crusade evangelism; however, the first night I heard Hank preach, I quickly realized how powerful the group approach really is. I had seen some of Billy Graham's big evangelistic crusades on television, and previously thought that was just emotionalism and peer pressure-type conversions that may not be very genuine, but personal involvement with our Rock Hill crusade made me realize that such thinking was just my critical spirit. We had two elder pastors who were on opposite ends of the denominational spectrum, and they were fairly opposed to the loud music being played in our little football stadium. One of them actually wanted to leave the stage in the middle of the field during the band's performance, but he held on to his ears and his seat, and it was a joy to see both of them ministering to people who had come forward to re-

Miracles Can Be Yours

ceive Christ after Hank's invitation. Then on the final evening of our crusade, *the entire York football team came forward*, and that was as genuine as it could have been, seeing most of those football players shedding real tears. I knew then that crusade evangelism was very effective.

It wasn't long after our Rock Hill crusade that Hank asked me to serve on his Board of Directors for the Hank Williams Evangelistic Ministries, and I certainly didn't have to pray about that very long before giving him an affirmative response. I had the privilege of participating in several more of his smaller town crusades, and that was his calling. Hank had discovered through a mentor's experience that an outreach in smaller towns was very effective and church follow-up was easier to organize than in larger cities.

Then came one of the more exciting times for our early family days, when Hank invited us to join his family for the Jamaica evangelistic crusade. Hank and I will never forget our youngest sons walking hand in hand down from the plane into the humidity of the Montego Bay Airport. Back then Jamaica did not have an air-conditioned walkway into the terminal. I also vividly remember that my wife insisted on having fried shrimp every day for lunch; it's amazing how we remember specific things on each trip. However, the most beautiful memory was seeing hundreds of those Jamaicans come forth each night as Hank would issue the invitation to receive Christ. There seemed to be a spirit of revival that encompassed Montego Bay, and even on the beach each day people were talking about Christ. Yes, even our oldest son made friends with a little boy his age, and was talking to him about Jesus on the beach.

It was absolutely an awesome experience to see my entire family involved in this crusade outreach, and it was like a little touch of heaven in a beautiful place. The airport runway was not far from our hotel, so the boys and I had a blast watching

10 – FAMILY EVANGELISM EXCURSION

the airplanes take off and land while we stood on a public walkway very close to the end of the runway. I told Hank about how the jet blast would literally blow us off the walkway down a few feet to the beach. He said, "If I can stand against Satan, I can stand against a 747," so I challenged him to come down with us; I have a picture of him *bracing for the jet blast*, and the next picture shows him *in the air headed toward the beach*! We also took a day excursion for a float down a lazy river on a raft, and then visited a beautiful waterfall. We all slept very well that final night.

    I think I left part of my heart there in Jamaica, and little did I know back then that I would be returning year after year to a place called Buff Bay and then Guys Hill, there in Jamaica, for dental/evangelistic outreach trips with different churches. It has truly been a blessing to see people's ear gates open, as extreme dental pain just melts away following a painless injection of anesthetic; yes, *faith comes by hearing* (Romans 10:17), and physical pain can block the ear gate.

Chapter 11
Another Divine Appointment

When I was attending Westminster Presbyterian Church in Rock Hill, we had a very popular Friday morning men's prayer breakfast. Sometimes 15 or 20 men would attend, and about five of the elder ladies prepared a wonderful, home-cooked breakfast for us. I remember one time we had homemade fig preserves, one of my favorites, and I asked the ladies if they bought those at Winn Dixie, a local supermarket. Well, sweet Hilda looked at me and said, "I made those." I gave her a big hug, and I told her, "I know; they're too good not to be homemade," and we both had a good laugh. After breakfast we normally had a devotional from various men in the church or a visiting missionary, and then had a prayer time. It was not unusual to have someone bring a visitor from time to time.

One Friday a fine-looking young man arrived, and no one introduced him as a guest. He was extremely quiet while we were having the meal, and he happened to be sitting right across from me, so I asked him what his name was; he stuttered through "Joel." I instantly knew that he had a major stuttering problem, just like I did when I was a boy. My dad was Wing Commander at Donaldson Air Force Base in Greenville, South Carolina, and I was required to answer the

11 – ANOTHER DIVINE APPOINTMENT

phone, "Colonel Fuller's residence, Noel Fuller speaking." I would stutter around trying to get "colonel" out, and invariably there would be a hang up resulting in my tears, and a run to Mommy. It took several years for me to overcome that major stuttering problem.

Joel looked to be about 20 years old, and I told him about my situation as a young boy, and that I knew exactly how he felt. With a big smile he seemed relieved and stuttered through "thank you," so I asked him if we could spend some time together after breakfast, and he nodded with another smile. Ironically, as we sang the first stanza of Amazing Grace, which was somewhat of a routine for us after breakfast, Joel seemed to have no problem singing! Fridays were normally my free day for catching up on paperwork, playing golf, or some other activity with the church, so I had plenty of free time that day, and so did Joel. We spent several hours together and he seemed comfortable struggling through his story, which was pretty amazing. At one point, I actually wondered if he was making it up; however, I could tell by his countenance that he was telling the truth.

Joel had grown up in Wisconsin, and he said the Lord had told him to come to JAARS; as you may remember, that is Jungle Aviation and Radio Service which was nearby in Waxhaw, North Carolina. When I asked him why he was in Rock Hill, he pulled out a map and showed me the little circle around Rock Hill that his parents had made on the map. As he was driving around Rock Hill that morning he saw all the cars at the church, and decided to see what was going on. I had the feeling I was dealing with a young man who had a tremendous amount of faith. He struggled through his testimony about how he had come to know the Lord as a young boy, and how he really wanted to be a missionary. Then he really surprised me with the fact that he had never been on a date with a girl. I was rather shocked, and asked, "Why not?" He stumbled through the fact that no one had ever said yes, so I told him that there was a great college here with lots of pretty girls, and that surely he could ask for a date by singing the question, as he had no problem singing. We both had a good laugh.

Joel and I became good friends, and I took him over to JAARS one day; he met with the aviation mechanics, and they were instantly impressed with his mechanical skills and testimony; the Lord opened the door for him to begin working there. Joel asked me a few weeks later if I could show him how to remove a tooth because he knew that one day it would be a skill he needed on the mission field. He had studied a good bit about missionary service, and knew that abscessed teeth were a major problem in third world countries. I told him that I did not extract many teeth, as I was an endodontist, and suggested that we take a mission trip together so I could show him how to remove a tooth. He seemed very receptive to that, and said he would look for a place that could accommodate that for us; we prayed several times that the Lord would open a door to that effect.

Within a couple of months, two amazing things happened: Joel had discovered a place in Colombia, South America that needed a dentist, and he had started dating a young lady at Winthrop University who could sing like a little songbird. I remember Joel telling me that he wanted his first kiss to be on his wedding day, and I knew then that he was a most unusual man.

As we all know, God always answers prayers that are in accordance with His will, so Joel and I found ourselves in a Wycliffe outpost called Loma Linda, in the middle of nowhere in Colombia, South America. Ironically, the same man who fixed the water line at Yarinacocha, Peru was to be a guide for

11 – Another Divine Appointment

Joel and me to go to the Dumi village, not far from the Loma Linda facility. While I was checking various missionaries' teeth at Loma Linda, I discovered an occlusal problem with one of the missionaries who had been having headaches every morning upon waking; her bite was hitting first on the right side of her mouth, which was causing temporomandibular problems on the left side, with resultant pain on the left side of her head. For 2 years she had been having headaches every morning, and she had been to Lima for a CT scan at their hospital, then back to the United States to see a neurologist, but no one could understand why she was having these headaches. I adjusted her right-side bite and she could tell an immediate difference in the way her teeth fit together evenly; the next morning she came by our guest house and hugged me several times, saying, "This is the first morning I have awakened without a headache." Needless to say, she was most appreciative.

Soon Joel and I were off in a small plane with our guide, on our way to a remote village that had never had a dentist, and we landed on a very primitive airstrip by a winding river. We were to go up the river several miles by boat; however, the motor for the boat would not start, so we had to hike to the village. I had a 60-lb. backpack full of dental supplies; fortunately, I was in marathon training, so I was in great shape. We were off through the jungle on a narrow trail that was about a foot deep in places because it was several generations old. Then we had to walk across some large logs placed in a line through a swamp, one foot right in front of the other, with the admonition, "Don't fall off because there are piranhas in the water!" We had a prayer, and then carefully crossed the 300-yard-long expanse with no problem. Then we were back on our 3-foot-wide trail through a dense jungle. The trail had forks in several places, but our teenage guide zipped right along, one foot right in front of the other, with the three of us trailing behind, wringing wet with sweat.

Then surprise of all surprises, a big Brahma bull was standing on the trail facing us, and there was not room for us to go into the dense jungle on each side, in order for the bull to come by! Our guide picked up a rock and threw it at the bull, but it just sailed over its head, and the bull snorted. Our guide said if he could hit the bull in the horns, it would turn around and run. I was thinking, "How in the world can that big bull turn around on this narrow trail?" I told him that I was a pretty good baseball pitcher, so let me have a try; I dropped my backpack, grabbed a wooden branch about 2 feet long, gave my best pitch, and slammed that bull right in the horns. Sure enough, the bull wheeled around, taking some of the trail with him, and took off.

It wasn't but a few more minutes, and we were into a pasture, as it was getting dark, and hiking up the hill to a small village. The people seemed most excited to see us, and had previously prepared THREE small fish, heads intact, for our dinner, along with some type of bread that tasted like Southern grits! The fish were cold, but I could have eaten all three! We dried off with a small towel in a little hut, changed clothes, had dinner, and, completely exhausted, climbed into our mosquito net hammocks. Unfortunately, some mosquitoes came in along with us, but we were too tired to be bothered with them. Fortunately, I was almost immune to their bites from my Peru trips. I awoke several times with the sound of pigs snorting around our open air hut; we must have had a very strange scent!

I could write two more chapters on our experiences there in the Dumi village of about 200 adults and 500 children, but I'll just wrap up with a quick synopsis here. The women

11 – ANOTHER DIVINE APPOINTMENT

walked each morning about a half mile down a hill to fill up their 5-gallon jugs of water for the day, and then back up the hill with the jugs on their heads. The children AND the adults loved bouncing my inflated latex gloves that I had blown up into large balloons and tied off; yes, they had never seen a balloon. Joel learned how to extract teeth rather proficiently, we got to experience an amazing medical miracle, which is another story in itself, and the New Testament of their heart language was delivered to them. They had a praise service for several hours in their small community worship hut, just singing their hearts out.

Then 2 days later, within just a few hours, with machetes they cleared a narrow runway strip for us in an open field, with waist-high brush, after we radioed a plane from Loma Linda to our location. We needed to take back a tiny, malnourished infant with a severe cleft palate, so we needed a plane to that location. The whole village, as well as neighboring ones, turned out to see the plane land, as rarely did they see or hear a plane in that area. I was amazed as they heard the engine of the plane almost 30 seconds before I could hear it, and I found out later that they could hear a cricket in a bush 100 yards away - no noise pollution there! Perhaps I will write another book one day, just about my experiences in the Dumi village, as EVERY DETAIL is still vivid in my mind's eye; what a blessing! Miracles have a way of making an indelible memory bank, which we can recall at will. I wish I could remember my patients' names that way, but that gift seems to be reserved for politicians!

When Joel and I got home, he came over for dinner one evening, and my son called him "The Bug Man," as he was still recovering from bug bites all over his arms and back! Joel wound up marrying his precious songbird, Robin, and their

Miracles Can Be Yours

first kiss was after the pastor proclaimed them husband and wife! They had two sons and served with Wycliffe in China as translators. Joel is now with the Lord, after an unexplained bout with cancer; some things we are not meant to understand. Yes, it is to the glory of God to conceal a matter, but that never negates the fact that we have an absolutely amazing, miracle-working God. See you next trip in Chapter 12.

Dr. Fuller, the young missionary dentist.

Chapter 12
To Russia with Love

Several years after the Jamaica crusade with the Hank Williams Evangelistic Ministries, I was invited to be part of their team for a Love Crusade to Russia; we did not take the Sean Connery movie *From Russia with Love*, but we did take the Russian translation of the *Jesus* film! There would be about 40 people involved in this crusade, and I only knew three of them: Hank Williams, his wife, Mary Ann, and the crusade director, Doug. I was to be the team doctor and bring various dental supplies, as dental outreach would be a valuable part of this crusade ministry. I'll never forget that when we all met in New York before our flight, I looked around and saw several rotund-looking people, and thought to myself, "I hope they don't get sick." They probably looked at me and thought to themselves, "I hope I don't get sick."

It was pretty phenomenal how the Lord bonded us together, as we had our initial prayer time there in the airport, and we had various gifts within the body of Christ represented, which were quite evident as we prayed together. It never ceases to amaze me that the best way to communicate with one another is through prayer. We had several very talented musicians and singers; one lady had purple hair, but she could sing like a songbird. I could not help but think about what the Russians

Miracles Can Be Yours

would think about this conglomerate group, and to my surprise, they loved our diversity.

The flight went very smoothly, but getting through customs with my dental supplies was a major issue, because of a language barrier. The customs officer was looking through my suitcase, and found numerous cans of carbocaine, an excellent anesthetic for tooth extraction. He asked me something in Russian, and when I had no response, he blew his whistle; immediately, three police agents came rushing over. I actually had to open one of the cans of carbocaine, put one of the little carpules into my syringe, put a needle on the end of it, and squirt the anesthetic into the air like a squirt gun. Then I opened my mouth and pretended the needle was to go into my mouth, saying, "Anestetica, numbing solution." Finally, they understood, and let me come through without confiscating what, I feel certain, they thought was cocaine. I did not have to use any of the anesthetic with our team, or at the revival, but when we went to a prison, that was a different story, which I will get to a little bit later in this chapter.

Moscow was an absolutely beautiful city with ancient buildings, compared to Washington, DC, and the streets were paved perfectly; however, by the time we were just 15 miles out of Moscow, on our way to Vladimir, the roads were in total disrepair. Telephone poles were down on the ground, and a few miles later, we found ourselves actually having to go around huge potholes in the road. Our very nice bus actually scraped the ground a few times, as we dipped into the corners of some of those potholes. I was shocked, but then realized there was very little traffic on the road; the people of Russia were not allowed to travel from city to city like we do in the US because most people had resident visas from the cities of their birth, and unless one was a gifted musician or talented athlete, one stayed in that city! When we arrived in Vladimir,

12 – TO RUSSIA WITH LOVE

which used to be the capital of Russia back in the EARLY days, it was encompassed almost entirely by a large river; yes, it was a natural moat back in the medieval days. We drove by a few churches that were actually built in the 600s, not 1600s!

Our hotel was a major shock, with very small rooms, and the bathroom was like a closet; one could actually sit on the toilet, take a cold water shower with a small rubber hose that had a ball of screen wire attached to the end as a shower head, and wash hands at a tiny sink, *all at the same time.* The toilet did have its own plumbing, but all other water exited through a hole in the middle of the floor. Needless to say, we took very quick showers! The hotel food was very good, but they put major attention on potatoes and cucumbers with very little meat.

There was a group of five translators who met with us for our first meal, and we seemed to be the only people in the restaurant. They explained to us that rarely did people stay in the hotel, the only one in Vladimir, as there was virtually no travel allowed between cities, even though the Iron Curtain had come down 2 years previously; however, it was still UP in Russia. One of our translators had served with the Billy Graham Evangelistic Ministry team that had been to Moscow the year before, and he seemed really excited about working with us. The first night of our crusade was in a large, beautiful theater, and people were packed into it, with very little standing room at the back; many were even outside listening to several loudspeakers. Hank delivered a wonderful message through our main translator, and many people came forward to receive Christ, with each one receiving a Bible.

Word spread very quickly all around Vladimir that the group from the United States had Bibles, and our beautiful bus became known as the *Bibla Bus*, as Bibla was their name for Bible. Each morning, after a breakfast of hard-boiled eggs

MIRACLES CAN BE YOURS

and cucumbers, we would pack the luggage areas of the bus with hundreds of Bibles, and then ride around, passing the Bibles out the windows as we were swamped at every intersection. Often the bus would be swarmed with people running up, hands in the air, crying "Bibla, Bibla!" Never before had I ever experienced such a hunger for the Word of God.

Each afternoon we would break up in groups of two or three people for day ministries at the three different hospitals, various orphanages, and the prison in Vladimir. I spent most of my time at each hospital showing the doctors how to use an aspirating syringe with my anesthetic carpules and disposable needles; I was shocked to find out that they had never even seen an aspirating syringe. At one of the hospitals they had a pint bottle of Novocain that had gone out of date in 1963! They kept it refrigerated in hopes that it would maintain its efficacy, and used it only in dire emergency situations. Most extractions, and even abdominal surgery, for that matter, were performed with Smirnoff vodka as sedation. Needless to say, I was stunned at the lack of equipment and anesthetic, but perhaps a better word would be *heartbroken*.

I got to know one of the dentists who could speak a little English, and he was a strong Christian. I wound up giving him all of my remaining anesthetic carpules, my syringes, and extraction forceps; he hugged me and wept with appreciation. Like most of the doctors, he had never even been to Moscow, which was only 200 kilometers away. One day I asked him if he was on salary, or if he was paid like I was, per procedure. He told me that every dentist in the three hospitals made $150 a month, and then he asked me, "How much do you make?" I told him that it really didn't matter how much, because it was all going to burn up one day, and we were both in agreement that we would take nothing to heaven with us but our faithfulness to obey the Lord. He said, "One day, we will all be

12 – TO RUSSIA WITH LOVE

rewarded for what we have done," and then added, "We must have the right motive, too," as he told me that he tried to share Christ with every one of his patients. I was convicted, because that was not my conviction – not yet!

As the week went by, each evening the crusade became more and more powerful, with several people being healed. Even our main translator was saved one evening while he was translating for Hank, and he continued on, without Hank speaking, to give the invitation to receive Christ. We ended up giving over 20,000 Bibles away, and at our evening reports, which were most uplifting, there were numerous reports of miraculous healing in the hospitals. The day I went to the jail, which was a life incarceration facility, some of our men were showing the Russian translation of the *Jesus* film, while I went to a small room to help the inmates who were in dental pain. The nurse at that facility would literally snap teeth with a pair of wire cutters so the abscesses could drain, leaving the inmate with just a dull toothache for the rest of his life. A huge guard was watching over me while I anesthetized several patients at a time, and then brought them back individually to remove their abscessed roots. I had just a wooden chair, with one light bulb hanging over it, and a bucket to spit into as my suction machine. I remember that big man of a guard kept saying, "No pain?" and I would look at him, saying, "No pain!"

Word spread to some of the guards who had toothaches, and they came into the little hallway where patients were waiting, so I began removing teeth on the guards as well. After a couple of hours, an amazing thing happened: another big guard came in, saying, "DOCTOR, COME," motioning with his arm to come with him. I tried to explain to him that I had several patients anesthetized, but he kept saying, "Doctor, come!" He took me down several hallways, through a few locked doors, and into a room that was obviously exquisitely

Miracles Can Be Yours

furnished and had beautiful hardwood walls that contained numerous plaques, pictures, and other memorabilia. The guard looked at me, extended his handshake, and said, "Stay!"

In the middle of the room was a small table, which was set for three for lunch. As I was looking around the room at the various pictures, in came one of our translators and a large man in his two-star Russian uniform. Introductions were made, and our translator told me that the general was the head officer at this prison of over 2,000 inmates. Little did I know that he had been watching the *Jesus* film, and he asked me through our translator, "Why did you come?" so I told him, "To help people." Then he said, "Does your government pay you?" and about that time the Holy Spirit took charge! I told him, "No sir, I am NOT paid; when you ask Jesus to take charge of your life, you do things that you wouldn't normally do," and our translator shared that with him. Immediately, I went on to say, "But more importantly, when Jesus takes charge, you're able to say NO to the things that are natural to a man." He responded by asking, "What do you mean?" He was a very handsome man about my age, so I asked him, "Do you have a problem with women?" He asked, "How do you know?" so I responded, "Because you are a man." Instantly, tears appeared in his eyes, and he asked, "How can I have your Jesus?"

As the Lord had ordained, before we even had the first bite of our lunch, we were on our knees, as I had the privilege of leading this powerful man, very slowly and deliberately, in the simple words of a Spirit-directed salvation prayer. We all laughed and cried afterwards as we hugged. I asked him why he wanted to speak to me rather than our crusade director. He simply said, "I wanted to talk to the smart man." I guess he figured, in his human wisdom, if I was a doctor, I was smart. God knew, in His infinite wisdom, exactly what that man needed to hear, and he put those words into my mouth; it had nothing

12 – TO RUSSIA WITH LOVE

to do with intelligence, just simple obedience. That day in the jail, the Lord impressed upon me so indelibly that I needed to begin helping people who were helpless and hopeless, regarding their dental problems, and I began praying for the Lord to open the door to areas where people fit that description.

Shortly thereafter, my physician, Dr. Eric Johnson, who had grown up on the mission field, called me to say, "I see that Kijabe Hospital in Kenya had an endodontist last month." Eric had gone to school there at the Kijabe complex, and he encouraged me to look into a mission trip with the Africa Inland Mission (AIM). Kenya was a predominantly English-speaking country, even though it had 42 different languages, and it seemed to fit the bill perfectly for hopeless, helpless people. Not surprisingly, the Lord opened the door for me to partner with the AIM, but not before I was "sifted like wheat" (Luke 22:31).

Unfortunately, most Christians, at some point in their process of sanctification, are tested by the Lord through one or more temptations of Satan, or merely drawn away by the deception of the world with its lust of the flesh, the pride of life, or the deceitfulness of riches. I have a good friend in Charlotte, NC, who says, "Men think that women have a PMS problem, but it is a male problem, with Pride, Money, or Sex; one or all three will bring a man down." Just looking through the men of the Scriptures, very few made it through as godly men without a major fall, and some were "shipwrecked in their faith" (1 Timothy 1:19). Most certainly, I was not exempt, and the next chapter, before we go to Kenya, is perhaps the most important one in this book, other than the *Up Close and Personal* of Chapter 8.

Chapter 13
Subtle Deception and Distraction

The major spiritual problem with deception is that, most of the time, one does not even know how or when he or she is being deceived. Almost like a chronically abscessed tooth, with NO symptoms, deception can keep one's physical energy level impaired, and it can steal one's joy and witness in the spiritual realm. As a trusting person, being deceived certainly was one of my major problems, and it came on so very insidiously over a period of many years; fortunately for me, it was diagnosed and treated effectively, but not after tormenting me for almost FOUR decades.

This chapter will be somewhat of a confessional to total strangers, and I must say that I'm a little uncomfortable right now, even proceeding with the matter, but I pray that it will keep someone from falling into the same trap that had me bound for years, even AFTER my salvation encounter with the Lord in 1980. It was almost a destructive force in my marriage, and ultimately had me tempted with suicidal thoughts from time to time; the absolutely insane part of it was that I thought everything was normal. For certain, pride, selfishness, bitterness, unforgiveness, and a host of soul ties with demonic forces can be powerfully destructive spiritual agents, gradually and methodically eating away at one's soul, just like

13 – Subtle Deception and Distraction

an abscessed tooth can eat away bone, or cancer can eat away vital internal organs with disastrous consequences. And TODAY, we have many Christians who are "weak, sick, and some sleep" (1 Corinthians 11:30), all because of deception or willful disobedience regarding communion. Yes, God still has a death angel, as He is "the same yesterday, today, and forever" (Hebrews 13:8).

It is now a proven medical fact that bitterness and unforgiveness can weaken one's immune system. Every week in my dental office I see patients with undiagnosed, chronic, asymptomatic, abscessed teeth, which means *no one knows about it and it does not hurt*, and these patients have no clue that there is a major problem brewing. This type of infection can flare up *overnight into an acute, sometimes very painful, infection* when the immune system becomes weakened; that can happen because of the flu, poor sleep, stress that becomes distress, a fight with the person's spouse, or numerous other situations that weaken the immune system. Yes, if your stress level goes up, your immune system goes down; I have seen it happen hundreds of times during my specialty years in endodontics, and the problem seems to be more prevalent as we are keeping our teeth longer into older age.

I will never forget the 82-year-old man who came in with painful swelling under his nose, and one of his front upper teeth was dark. Normally, as we age the canal spaces in our roots get smaller, resulting in slightly darker teeth, and less sensitivity to cold – one benefit of the golden years! However, when I took an X-ray of this man's front teeth, his darker front tooth had a large abscess at the end of the root, and a *10-year-old-size canal space*; the other teeth had normal canal space closure. I asked him if he had been hit in the face as a boy. He said, "Yeah, a baseball hit me in the mouth, the tooth got dark after that, but it never hurt until last night." So that

MIRACLES CAN BE YOURS

tooth was traumatized when he was young, yet 70 YEARS LATER he got a cold, and the infection, *which had been dormant for most of his life*, went BOOM. That is the longest period of time I have seen an abscess just smolder, but 15 or 20 years is not uncommon after an elbow in the face at a high school basketball game, an auto accident, or a head bump from a young child while playing. An abscess might smolder, too, if a partial root canal procedure, just to get someone out of pain, is not completed; years later a severe infection can surface, which often requires surgical intervention. Often the chronic abscess must be removed surgically, along with the tooth, if the root has fractured.

Amazingly, the SAME THING can happen in our spiritual lives when we have experienced emotional or spiritual trauma, and it can lie dormant for years, with a sinful attitude covered by the deception of pride! Unfortunately, a simple, "Forgive my shortcomings," does not take care of the *root cause* of the deep, smoldering problem or problems! Yes, I'll say it again, deep wounds require deep cleansing!

Looking back *on my personal life*, just about every December, after my college years, I would usually come down with a terrible cold, which would often turn into a debilitating bronchitis or laryngitis. Not many years ago, I was *finally able to realize* that it was the smoldering disappointment and almost hatred that I had toward God regarding my father's painful death on December 7, 1969. At the time, I was not a Christian, and I was literally infuriated with God because of the agonizing way in which my dad died, overdosed on morphine, and wasting away to 87 pounds before his death. Cancer can be an insidiously evil event, and I feel certain that the *origin of some cellular rebellion* can be spiritual in nature, and *if the root cause of that rebellion is not removed*, clinical cancer, in all of its various manifestations, can surface. If chronic physical or chemical irritation

13 – SUBTLE DECEPTION AND DISTRACTION

can cause cancer, perhaps *sustained bitterness and unforgiveness* can do the same.

My dad never spoke about the Korean Conflict, probably because of the internal pain and anger he experienced because of that political event, as was Vietnam's political quagmire. So many of our finest young men in the military who go to battle have come home physically and mentally crippled. Perhaps that is why we have so many of our veterans TODAY committing suicide, because of *the deception of the real enemy*; not ISIS, but the Devil and his demonic spirits! If I had not put a praise tape in my car one day, I may have been one of those casualties, too, *and that happened AFTER I had surrendered to Christ!* Yes, I already had planned out the bridge abutment that I was going to take my Suburban into at 70 mph, with my cell phone in my hand! SO, how can that happen? The answer is *subtle deception*! Perhaps that is why we have so many pastors TODAY dropping out of the ministry; *spiritual warfare coming from within*; and, of course, some of our seminary graduates are truly *wolves in sheep's clothing!*

I am now convinced that my *anger and resentment* every December, following 1969, weakened my immune system to the point that I got a cold. God says, "The anger of man never achieves the righteousness of God" (James 1:20), and, medically speaking, a deep wound requires deep cleansing. So, as a new Christian in 1980, those things are supposed to be resolved, right? I have shocking news for many pastors who think that demonic spirits cannot abide in a Christian. I was indeed a new creation and all things had become new (2 Corinthians 5:17), but unfortunately, the garbage of the previous 10 years was still inside my mind; yes, demonic spirits were residing inside my body. Those spirits, and they are demonic spirits of hate, resentment, anger, frustration, etcetera, were just like a smoldering abscessed tooth, waiting for an appro-

Miracles Can Be Yours

priate *weakened time to explode with acute venom*. Often my own *chronic spiritual infection* would manifest with a verbal outburst upon the ones I loved the most, my family.

    I firmly believe that new Christians, especially those who are saved later in life, who have been exposed to tragic events prior to salvation, can experience real psychogenic pain, which needs special care. Furthermore, those who have thoroughly entrenched worldly strongholds, various types of visual entertainment habits — pornography, to be specific — or those who have experimented with the world of recreational drugs, and the demonic forces that go along with them, need SPECIAL attention. Often they need to go through a deliverance period where REAL DETAILED confession, forgiveness, repentance, and restitution where appropriate, can take place. Yes, let's not forget restitution where stealing is a problem. Such was the case with me in 2007, as I had never made APPROPRIATE confession, repentance, and restitution in many areas for my past sins, and, unfortunately for me, they were still active in my mind, covered with a thick layer of PRIDE, which became thicker the more I learned about religion's C/R switch: confess and repent became compromise and rationalize.

    Although I received the Lord's salvation through the evangelical outreach of a conservative church, from my perspective, their main emphasis was on the intellectual aspect of faith and grace, rather than repentance. Unfortunately, knowledge has a tendency to *subtly puff one up* into a state of *unrecognized pride*. I was certainly full of that pride, in its various forms, and, ironically, it became a more powerful, deceptive force in my life the more Scripture I memorized. I often tell people that there are four main pride words: I, mine, time, and fine. Yes, when I control what is mine in accordance with my time plan and I think I'm fine, I'm actually *in a real mess*. Plenty of *successful people* all around the world are in that state of deprav-

13 – Subtle Deception and Distraction

ity, which usually leads to *various forms of greed*. The password for greed is just four letters: M O R E !

In 1990 I was on top of the world with a beautiful wife who poured quality time into me and our two precious boys, ages 7 and 2 at the time, a dental practice that was booming, a new business corporation with a built-in profit sharing plan and family-limited partnership that was going to lead to an easy life down the road; yes, I was following the world's system for success. I was active in dental associations on the state and national level, a deacon in my church, taught our Evangelism Explosion training program, a leader in our Pioneer Boys program, on the Salvation Army board, active in prison ministry, on the Hank Williams Evangelistic Ministries board, faithfully attended Wednesday night prayer meetings and Thursday morning prayer breakfasts, and attended just about every spiritual enrichment program I could find like Bill Gothard seminars, Promise Keepers events, James Robinson retreats in Texas, numerous marriage enrichment weekends, and more, ad nauseam. And then, just to stay in touch with my worldly desires, I enjoyed deer hunting in the fall season, turkey hunting in the spring season, coaching Little League baseball, playing golf in the summer, fishing, camping with the boys, training runs for marathons, and on and on. So, most psychologists and unknowing people would say that I had burnout, but NO, it was a very subtle, insidious, deceptive satanic attack, inside my very soul, and I had no idea it was taking place, nor that I was actually opening doors for demonic forces to control me, by the very complaining and critical words that were coming out of my mouth.

Yes, God says, "The power of life and death lies in the tongue" (Proverbs 18:21). I even paid a professional counselor for weeks, only to hear him say, "That is not good; pray for mercy." Simple spiritual warfare defense tactics were of little

MIRACLES CAN BE YOURS

significance in my attempts to ward off this activity, and numerous prayer and fasting attempts were like putting a Band-Aid on an active infection. Basic first aid teaches that the wound cleansing must first take place, before covering it with a medicated dressing, and I had tried all kinds of dressing that actually pushed my wounds deeper into my very being. You may think this sounds a little ridiculous and even scary, but it turned out to be, as my mother would say, "as real as the nose on my face."

I pray that you have never been where I was, and perhaps you haven't, if you were saved at an early age. Personally, I think the strongest testimony is one that says, "I have been serving the Lord who has kept me from all the garbage of the world since my young age." Certainly the Lord can save anyone who comes to Him when He draws him to Jesus by the Holy Spirit, and He has used drug addicts who have been murderous criminals in powerful ways. Furthermore, our deepest hurts often become our most effective ministries; however, some superficial converts can slide back into old demonic habits, if a genuine confession and spiritual cleansing have not taken place. That may be why our recidivism rate is so high in prison salvation experiences. Certainly, if the trash space in a person's life is not filled with the Holy Spirit, the trash can come back with 7 more friends (Matthew 12:45) and the person is worse off than before (2 Peter 2:20, 21). To the shame of superficial Christian counseling, that catastrophe is thoroughly documented.

I could have possibly gone that route, but PRAISE GOD, in HIS perfect timing, He provided a friend who knew how to help me, and I have two rather worn pieces of paper in my Bible that document a deliverance session in my home, with him and his wife, one evening. It started at 6:20 PM, on February 13, 2007, and ended at 9 PM. During that almost 3-hour

13 – SUBTLE DECEPTION AND DISTRACTION

session, 32 demonic spirits came out of my body. Most pastors will say that demons can't live in a Christian, but I know for a fact that a host of them came out of my tears, nose, mouth, and stomach. I was not possessed, but I was certainly oppressed, and I have the firm conviction that many in the body of Christ have a similar problem – deceptive demonic oppression! Once again, demons are really just disembodied spirits looking for a body to occupy or harass, and they come in through various gates: 9 of them. More on that later!

Perhaps that is why so many Christians are joyless and weakly effective when it comes to fulfilling the Great Commission. Yes, the final words of our Lord are *clear as a bell*, and yet, how many of us even know what He said, much less, *fulfill His command*. Perhaps, just perhaps, it is because we have an inhibiting force that lives within us along with His precious Holy Spirit. Yes, we have spirits of deception and distraction running rampant on the earth today, even among Christians. I personally know of three pastors who actively ran Ponzi-type schemes under the auspices of Christian ministry and financial prosperity. Unfortunately, it was my *spirit of greed, and it is a spirit,* that got me personally involved with all three of those pastors, none of whom is in Rock Hill. Since that time, I have learned a wonderful truth from the Word of God: "There is one who makes himself rich, and yet has nothing; and there is one who makes himself poor, and yet has great riches" (Proverbs 13:7) which goes right along with "Righteousness and contentment are a means of great gain" (1 Timothy 6:6).

Yes, we seem to put a dollar sign on riches, don't we? These days we seem to measure success with dollars or with numbers, and think that *bigger is better, and more is good or best*. I tried that philosophy on several occasions, and it almost turned out to be a destructive curse, just like the Bible says it can be. For certain, God can send upon someone a deluding influence so

MIRACLES CAN BE YOURS

that he will believe that which is false (2 Thessalonians 2:11), and that is a scary place to be. Yes, *deception and mental depravity* seem to be getting more and more prolific. I pray that you never go there, because there can be a point in time when one can be broken, without remedy, and God will laugh at your calamity. Please check out the latter third of Proverbs 1 if you don't believe me.

If, by chance, you have found yourself in a lukewarm state, or if you have lost your first love, Christ Jesus, please, please get with someone who knows about *true repentance and restitution*, and make things right with the Lord. You will be forever grateful for *the real freedom, gratitude, and joy* that will bubble up within you. Money can never buy peace; in fact, peace is not for sale! The peace of God and the joy of the Lord is His gift to you for your *simple obedience to His word out of an attitude of gratitude for what He has done for you*. So, bottom line: Are you in the Word of God on a daily basis, looking for practical application, or are you more inclined to spend most of your time behind the idiot box — the television — or other forms of personal entertainment? Interestingly, the root word for entertain means to strangle or choke! Furthermore, in today's world we have numerous forms of distraction that will minimize our effectiveness. From time to time we need to do a self-inventory on our ability to concentrate, and how effectively we can communicate. Yes, there are spirits out there that deceive and distract – that is their sole purpose.

My purpose in this chapter is not to offend, but to enlighten with the truth of my life, and my heart cry is to motivate you to a closer walk with Jesus Christ, and ultimately, to become His disciple. That cannot happen if the root cause of your past sin has not been cut, and sometimes that can be a painful experience. Jesus said, "IF you are my disciples, you

13 – Subtle Deception and Distraction

shall know the truth, and the truth will set you free" (John 8:31-32). However, *that is another BIG IF.* So, here's to freedom!

You'll meet a good friend of mine from Guyana, South America in a few chapters, and I think he summarizes this entire chapter into a simple truth: "God won't pour His love into your cup if there is willful trash in the bottom." Nor can we cover that trash with deceptive demonic spirits, with good works or pride. So, here's to REAL freedom; please receive it, as you take a daily shower in the truth of His Marvelous Word. We wash the outside of our bodies, but we sometimes neglect washing the inside, and often we let a subtly deceptive enemy inside our eye gates, ear gates, nose gates, or mouths, yes 7 of the 9 gates are in our head! Once these enemies are in, they MUST be cleaned out, and replaced with the Holy Spirit. So, here's to our daily shower! After that, if our thoughts don't line up with the fruit of the spirit (Galatians 5:22), then we are under the deception of the Kingdom of Darkness, and we may need some professional help. Often *it takes another person to detect our blind spots*, and accountability is *only as effective as our truthfulness*. More on that later! Let's take a break for some laughter – good medicine! (Proverb 17:22).

Chapter 14
Bass Ackwards to Kenya

I thought this title might catch your attention, especially after the serious nature of our last chapter; humor is always a great way to transition, or to diffuse anger. I pray that the last chapter did not generate any unnecessary anger – *perhaps conviction* – but not anger, unless it is directed toward evil in our souls, and we certainly need to turn the tables on that matter. Yes, we are to "hate evil with a perfect hatred" (Psalms 139:21; Proverbs 8:13, 29:27). When God talks about something three times, we need to really pay attention! Furthermore, it is OK to be angry, "but don't let your anger result in sin, or even let the sun go down on our anger;" don't want to "give the Devil a foothold" (Ephesians 4:26) on us, do we? All right, that is enough preaching for one paragraph!

One of my dad's favorite humorous expressions was *bass ackwards*, and he used it frequently, along with several others. It is amazing we all remember little verbal innuendos and crazy expressions from our parents, and quite often use them ourselves, as they get passed down from one generation to the next, as do our sin nature and strongholds (Exodus 20:5). Thankfully these curses can be broken by the blood of Christ. This little *bass ackwards* expression just happened to pop into mind, as I am recalling my first trip to Kenya. If you ever go there, you

14 – Bass Ackwards to Kenya

will probably leave part of your heart in that country, just like I did, and I wound up going back five different times.

Most of my early mission trips were via American Airlines, primarily because of a direct flight from Charlotte, North Carolina to Miami or Dallas/Fort Worth, and then direct flights to various places in South America and Mexico, so I had developed somewhat of a loyalty to American Airlines. However, when I called them about flying to Kenya (that's back when you had to make all of your reservations by phone), the agent's recommendation for my particular time schedule was a direct flight from Charlotte to Dallas/Fort Worth, then a direct flight to London, where British Air would take me to Kenya. I asked the agent, "Isn't that a little bass ackwards?" Her reply was, "Excuse me!" I apologized for the slang expression, which obviously caught her off guard, and asked, "Why would I want to fly west for 2 hours, wait for 2 more hours, and then turn around and backtrack the path that I had just flown?" She explained that my air miles were not available for that time period to New York, so their Dallas hub would be the route I would need to take. I thanked her and told her that I would look for a better route.

So I checked the yellow pages (remember those handy little things before Google came about?), and I found an 800 line for British Air. Sure enough, they had a direct flight from Raleigh, North Carolina to London for a very reasonable price, and that was well worth the 3-hour drive to Raleigh, rather than the *asinine* (there's another one from Dad) 2+-hour flight, 2-hour layover in Dallas/Fort Worth, and then backtracking in the air for 2 more hours!

While I'm talking about booking flights, which used to be somewhat of a tedious undertaking, the following year British Air had a direct flight out of Charlotte to London, which was very convenient. Unfortunately, the third year, they must have

Miracles Can Be Yours

been breaking in their St Louis connector, with a direct flight to London, as that was their only option to London, other than Chicago or New York. I learned two valuable lessons on that particular trip: never take a tempting *first class upgrade* when they are going to change your estimated time of arrival (ETA) by more than 3 hours, and never fly *without a change of clothes* in your carry-on bag! While waiting for the St Louis departure, an announcement was made regarding two *first class passengers* on the Chicago to London flight who were willing to exchange their primo tickets for seats on the St Louis departure; they obviously needed to get to London ASAP. The Chicago flight would involve a 4-hour delay. I had time to spare, and I had never flown first class on a big jet, so out of curiosity, I was one of the two passengers who took advantage of the free upgrade, and opted for the detour to Chicago.

Following an amazing first class flight to London on a 747, which was right on schedule about 4 hours behind my originally ticketed St Louis flight arrival, no checked bags came through for me in the pickup area. Oops, British Air had not transferred either passenger's free upgrade bags to the Chicago-bound flight out of St Louis. We might as well have been in a foreign country, as a man from Texas and another from South Carolina were trying to communicate with these British blokes at the baggage claim area. Needless to say, it was rather *bass ackwards*, with communication efficiency, and even I had trouble understanding this cowboy from Texas, so I knew the Brits were at a total loss. Neither of us had claimed our bags within British Air's 3-hour time limit for passenger bag pickup, and no one seemed to know where they were; we were sent to the lost baggage claim area.

A very nice British Air agent told me, "I say, mate, perhaps they were transferred over to your departure terminal for tomorrow's flight" in a typical jovial British formal tone. So I

14 – Bass Ackwards to Kenya

told him in my Southern voice, "Sir, they told me in Charlotte to be SURE and get my bags in London, as my layover was too long for a bag transfer." His response was, "I beg your pardon?" I tried to speak very clearly in what I thought was very understandable English, but this fellow still could not get past my Southern drawl. He said, "No problem, mate; just be sure to be at the other terminal 2 hours before your flight tomorrow morning."

Mr. Cowboy and I parted ways, as we wished each other good luck, and I got a taxi over to my sweet Aunt Sheila's new townhouse, which was just 20 minutes from Heathrow Airport. She was worried, and very upset that I hadn't called her, because I was several hours behind schedule, and she began to fuss, but immediately she was overshadowed by a screaming noise. She grabbed me by the hand, pulling me outside, saying, "Oh, my darling, you must see this!" I literally had to cover my ears as the amazing Concord jet flew directly overhead. Aunt Sheila asked, "Isn't it absolutely marvelous?!" but I was horrified by the decibel level of those engines. I asked her, "How often does this happen?" She replied, "Oh, just twice a day. You missed the first one; isn't it just magnificent?" She took me by the hand again, saying, "Now let's go back inside and I'll make a pot of tea; you must be exhausted." I thought to myself, "Thank you, Lord, for the perfect timing of that jet," as there was no more fussing about me not calling her.

We had a wonderful visit and it was early to bed for this Southern man, as I had an early flight to catch in the morning. Aunt Sheila came with me to the airport, just in case I needed a translator with these British blokes. Lo and behold, my bags were sent back to the US the evening before, but "Not a problem; they will be on their way to Kenya as soon as possible!" Little did I know, their *soon as possible* would be about as *bass ackwards* as American Airlines trying to talk me into an unnec-

Miracles Can Be Yours

essary Dallas/Fort Worth flight leg and back across the same path, 3 years before this debacle.

Of course, when I got to Kenya after an 8-hour flight, my contact with the Africa Inland Mission (AIM) was surprised that I was traveling with just one carry-on bag. I checked with the baggage official, as London had advised, and they had no word on my checked bags! It took 9 DAYS for them to arrive, just in time for my departure from Kenya. Unfortunately for me, British Air had sent my bags all the way back to Charlotte, North Carolina, and it took a week for *slow-moving Carolina* to figure out what had happened. Have you ever tried to dry a pair of hand-washed underwear in 40-degree weather? It is winter time in Kenya in July! Have you ever tried to put damp 40-degree underwear on your nice warm body? I learned the second night to forgo the outside clothes line, wash my one pair of underwear in hot water, roll it in a dry towel after a good squeeze, and then perform a slow spin in front of the fireplace for about 20 minutes to dry it. Now that you have the routine, I pray that you never have to use it!

One final blessing was that British Air flew me home from Kenya with a *complimentary business class seat*. I never again took a *free first class seat upgrade* involving a plane change, and probably never will. However, in today's world the airlines must be certain that EVERY passenger accompanies his or her checked bags for security purposes. One time, 7 years ago, coming home from Tel Aviv, our flight departure was delayed almost 2 hours because there was a bag on board without an accompanying passenger. It was a tedious, time-consuming task finding it, unpacking the cargo boxes on the runway, but no one seemed upset. Before takeoff, it was announced that it was a bomb! Thank the Lord for the diligence of Tel Aviv officials on that day, or you may not be reading this right now!

14 – Bass Ackwards to Kenya

If you ever get the opportunity to go to the Holy Land, please don't pass it up; it is, indeed, the Promised Land, with phenomenal security technology. Yes, here's praying that you received a little humor out of this short chapter. The next one will be back to the miraculous sovereign power of our Lord on my first flight from London to Nairobi; it was another divine appointment in the air!

Chapter 15
London to Nairobi and Beyond

One never knows what the Lord has in store for a disciple of Christ when he or she boards an airplane, especially when it comes to being a faithful witness. *Praying for a divine appointment* is the first step to creating an opportunity for witness, especially when there is an 8-hour flight on one's agenda. I know a couple of people who have a true phobia about flying, and would never even think about getting on a plane. I know others who board a plane with a sense of fear, mostly because of a bad experience with severe turbulence or some other unpleasant experience on a previous flight. There are others who fly frequently and board with ease, just like they do when getting into their cars for pleasant drives, even though the highways can be among the most dangerous places in the world. However, there are a few who board a plane with *anticipation regarding the opportunity* to have a good conversation with a stranger. It is my privilege to fall into that category.

As is my habit, especially before a long flight, my Bible is usually in my lap as the plane taxis out to the main runway for takeoff, and I am normally reading a Proverb or one of the Psalms. On a certain day in June, back in the year 2001, I was on a night flight on a big British Air plane to Nairobi, Kenya. I was in the aisle seat, which is my preference on long flights so

15 – LONDON TO NAIROBI AND BEYOND

I can easily get up and stroll about from time to time. The seat beside me was vacant, and a lady about my age was in the window seat. I knew from my mom's British nature and a couple of trips to London in previous years, that the British people were not hesitant to strike up conversations with strangers.

So I was not surprised when the lady in the window seat asked, "Is that the Bible?" I responded, "Yes, ma'am, it is." Her next question was, "So you are a man of the cloth?" "Oh, no, ma'am, I am a dentist." "You are a dentist, and you read the Bible?" "Yes, ma'am, don't you read the Bible?" "Why, NO, I'm Anglican!" I knew right then, from personal experience with my mom and Aunt Sheila, that I did not need to ask any further questions about her spiritual condition, so I just read my Bible as the plane took off, and prayed for discernment. As we reached altitude and leveled out, I put my Bible in the seat pocket in front of the vacant seat between us, and asked her, "Are you visiting family in Kenya?" "No, I'm a botanist, and I'm going to study some unusual flowers in the Rift Valley area." "That is interesting; this is my first trip to Kenya, and I understand there is an amazing variety of plants, animals, and birds in Kenya." "Oh, yes, Kenya is a marvelous place. I've been there many times with my husband to study; are you doing some dental work?" "Yes, ma'am, I'm hoping to work with some of the primitive people groups in the Nairobi area." She seemed a little surprised, and asked, "Does the Kenyan government pay you for your work?" "No, ma'am, I just enjoy helping people who are hopeless and helpless."

Then she asked me something that told me where her heart was: "Why wouldn't you want to be paid?" About that time a nice meal arrived and we enjoyed that with some silence. As I put my napkin on my tray, I was not surprised to hear her ask, "You Americans always eat so fast; why is that?" "I don't know; I guess it's because we're always in such a hurry." As she was finishing up her meal in such a proper British fashion, I sensed in my spirit that she was probably an evolutionist, as well as a stubborn Anglican. I told her that I knew a little bit about evolution in the animal kingdom and embryonic recapitulation, but that I knew very little about the plant kingdom. So I asked her, "I sense that you are an expert in botany; could you tell me how a pine tree became an oak?" "Oh, my, that is most intriguing." "Or how a daffodil became a rose?" "Why, I have never really contemplated that!" So I calmly explained to her that the Bible was very clear about God making the fish and their kind, and the birds and their kind, and that is why one can't mate a bird with a fish. Her question was, "Is that really what the Bible says?"

I knew in my spirit that the Holy Spirit was opening a door for an effective witness, so I reached into the seat pocket and pulled out my Bible, turning to Genesis and showed her that God made sea creatures, animals, and birds, and their kind. She sounded just like my Aunt Sheila when she said, "Oh, my!" Then I told her that Jesus had actually made everything, turning to the New Testament to show her where Paul had said, "All things were made by Him and for Him, and in Him all things were held together" (Colossians 1:16). Then I flipped to the Gospel of John and asked her, "Would you like to read about Jesus, and who He really is?" and offered her the Bible. When she took it, I began praying as she read. Not surprisingly, just a couple of minutes later, she looked over at me with tears in her eyes, and said, "I didn't know that Jesus was God!" "Yes, my dear mother, who was also Anglican, did not know that either, until just 2 months before her death; would you like to hear about that?" I showed her a picture of the two of us that was in my Bible cover. She said, "Yes, I would like to hear about that very much."

15 – London to Nairobi and Beyond

Needless to say, in about 20 minutes, this precious lady was praying to receive Christ, and not long after that, she was sound asleep with the peace of God enfolding her. I was so exhilarated that it took me about an hour to go to sleep, but I slept soundly for the remainder of our flight. The captain's announcement that we were preparing to land probably awakened both of us at the same time, and as we descended into Nairobi, this precious new Christian beside me opened her window shade to show me the glorious 200-mile visibility that was consistently predictable in Kenya. She said, "I had some wonderful dreams on the flight; is that one of the blessings of being a new Christian?" I told her she would be very surprised regarding how *all things would become new* (2 Corinthians 5:17). She shared with me that her husband was Kenyan, and would be meeting her at the airport; she insisted that I take the time to meet him.

I knew all about the British way of insistence, so I told her that meeting him would be my pleasure, especially since I had never met a Kenyan. She was so excited, and told me that he was a new Christian, but she was just too stubborn to listen to him. Then she said that the last thing he told her before she left for England to lecture at the university was that he would be praying for her ears to be opened! Yes, prayer has a more powerful force than we can possibly even imagine. The Lord says, "I can do exceedingly abundantly, beyond what you can ask or think" (Ephesians 3:20-21).

After we cleared customs it was a delight for me to watch this lady run into her husband's arms, with a new kind of love for him. They spoke for just a few minutes, hugged each other again, and then she introduced me to him. I could tell immediately that he was a sweet, caring man, as he shook my hand, and then gave me a big Kenyan hug. He said, "Jambo, so you are the man that God used; welcome to your new

Miracles Can Be Yours

home." We chatted just a few minutes, and then he said something that surprised me: "You must be a very patient man to get my wife's attention." I told him that actually I was a fairly impatient person outside an airplane, and that I just watered with the Word of God the seed that he obviously had planted. Then he asked, "But how did you get her to read the Bible?" I told him that I just sparked her curiosity about how the daffodil could become a rose. He thanked me again and asked me where I was going. I told him it was a strange-sounding place, as I looked into my Day Timer, saying, "They told me to call this number and ask for transport to a place called Kijabi." He said, "Please put that notepad away; we are going right by there, and will save you some time."

As we left the airport together, I looked out into this huge expanse of a field and saw a giraffe, pointed with my finger, which my wife does not like me to do, and said, "Look, there's a giraffe!" They both chuckled and said, "Yes, you are in Africa now, and you haven't seen anything yet." Ironically, I said the exact same thing to my son 4 years later when Pam and Mike came with me to Nairobi. How amazing it is when the Lord gives us some little déjà vu experiences! Now Pam and I are going through some amazing déjà vu experiences with our two grandsons, taking us back 33 years, with vivid memories regarding our little Sam. Ironically, Lord willing, in *just a few months* this 2016, I will be taking Sam and Mike to Africa for a first-time safari! Yes, He is an amazing Lord! Perhaps you will be reading this at the same time we are in that magnificent place.

I have had the privilege of seeing firsthand just about every continent except Antarctica, and I have no desire to go there at my age. However, I am very excited about seeing and hearing *the new earth*; the Lord has said, "Eye has not seen nor ear heard the things that He has in store for us!" (1 Corinthians 2:9). If that does not give us powerful motivation to live

15 – LONDON TO NAIROBI AND BEYOND

for Him, I don't know what will, *or something may be wrong with your motor*! (See Chapter 8 and/or 13.)

How miraculous it is that the Lord arranges just the right people to sit together on flights, just like the Peruvian who flew home with Rick and me from Lima, Peru. And how marvelous it is that He arranges every supernatural detail of our lives; if we could just "present every thought captive to His obedience" (2 Corinthians 10:5), things would run a lot more smoothly for us, and we would see His miraculous nature, just like Jesus did, *on a much more frequent basis*. The formula for success is very simple, "Seek first His Kingdom and His righteousness, and…" (Matthew 6:33); we often get consumed with the "…", and forget the prerequisite.

For certain, it is unfortunate that we live in such a way that we just get glimpses of the miraculous every now and then, but one glorious day, that will change. In the next few chapters I will share some of the miraculous things that I have been able to witness, and they were all evidenced in such a way that they *brought glory and praise to God*. I believe Satan can do miraculous things as well, and we'll probably see more of that *as the antichrist spirit becomes stronger* and more prevalent, but the true test for a real miracle is very simple: *Does the Lord receive glory and praise when it is performed*, or is it a man or woman who receives the praise? This is just some food for thought before we proceed. Please remember, when ordinary people like us, *peaceful people who are willing to share His Word in peace*, just like the Peruvian who flew home with Rick and me from Lima, Peru, it *produces a fruit of righteousness* (James 3:18), as he shared with his sister. See you back in Kenya next chapter!

Chapter 16
Clean Air and Real Christianity

Trying to cover five trips to beautiful Kenya is somewhat like trying to eat an elephant, but like they say, take it one bite at a time, so I'll get started. The first thing that struck me as purely magnificent about Kenya was the visibility, from my first glimpse out of the airplane window to my first evening sitting on the runway at Kijabe, a medical educational complex, 6,500 feet on a mountainside, overlooking the Great Rift Valley. Kijabe means *place of the wind*, and just about every afternoon the warm air from the Rift Valley would come up the mountainside and produce a wonderful afternoon breeze, sometimes upwards of 40 miles an hour.

My first day there, I was given a brief tour of the complex which included a wonderful hospital and dental clinic, a Bible College, the famous Rift Valley Academy, about 200 or so modest homes, and a small motel. The entire side of the mountain around this complex was dotted with very small houses, a few churches, and most of the roads were very rough dirt roads. The few roads that had asphalt which they called tarmac had numerous potholes, and the little road that went to their grass strip runway switch backed all the way down the mountainside to the Rift Valley where there was an orphanage.

16 – CLEAN AIR AND REAL CHRISTIANITY

My first evening there, I walked down to the little runway and looked out across the expanse of the Rift Valley, and I could see all the way to the other side, well over 200 miles away. There was a NASA tracking station about 60 miles out in the valley, and it looked like I could reach out and touch it. I had never seen visibility like that other than in Nepal when I was in the Navy back in 1974/75. As I sat on the end of that runway, there was a beautiful sunset, and I was surprised how quickly it started getting dark; yes, I was very close to the equator again. In fact, it was hard to see by the time I got to the dimly lit Kijabe complex about a mile away.

Kenya was 6 hours ahead of the U.S. east coast daylight savings time, and I found that jet lag flying from west to east is indeed a really challenging phenomenon. Our bodies definitely have built-in time clocks, and for 3 days I was ready for bed by 4:00 in the afternoon and wide awake at 2:00 in the morning, so I literally had to *make myself adapt* to the Kenyan time difference. Adaptation is certainly a necessary ability regarding the world system, and learning how to say "NO" can be a struggle for many. I like the Phillips translation of the Bible that says, "Don't let the world squeeze you into its mold" (Romans 12:2).

The next thing that struck me as refreshing as the visibility was the character of the people; they were spontaneously friendly, genuinely caring, obviously Christian people who were there to honor the Lord. More importantly, they understood the power of prayer and did not hesitate to use that power frequently. The *first thing the dental staff did each morning at the clinic* was to read the Scripture and pray, and that impacted me so greatly that we still do that today in our office in Rock Hill; we read a Psalm and pray. I made one of those *immediate friendship bonds* at the dental clinic with a young man named Duncan Odupoy; he was a Masai who spoke several of the

Miracles Can Be Yours

Kenyan languages fluently, and as the Lord would have it several years later, I had the privilege of sponsoring him through dental school in Uganda where he graduated in 2008. He is now an outstanding dentist in Nairobi, married to his beautiful Esther, and they now have three children; I am certain we will be lifelong friends.

The other person with whom I really clicked was Dr. Bruce Dahlman who was a missionary with the Africa Inland Mission (AIM). He would literally fly over the top of the potholes in his Toyota Land Cruiser, and had memorized the ones for which he needed to slow down. We went to many of the outlying primitive areas to minister medically and evangelistically to some of the unreached areas. I'll never forget the day we were on our way to the Delamere plantation, and he kept asking me numerous questions: "What do you think that is ahead in the distance? How far away is it? What do you think that is on the left side of that lake? How many do you think there are?" Those questions were all related to a lake that was about 70 miles away and contained a flock of 30,000+ flamingos! I was not very accurate with any of my immediate answers to his questions, and he really had me stumped on the flamingos, as I was thinking an oil slick glistening in the sun, then plankton, and, finally, acid rain! Yes, he was a brilliant physician with an innate ability to teach; in fact, he is still there doing a magnificent job.

I really thought that one day, if the Lord provided a buyer for my dental office in Rock Hill, I would wind up back in Kenya working with Bruce at Kijabe. The one time I did have a potential buyer, a Kenyan ministry team had committed to work with me, a website was established, and we had furniture for our office on site; that door closed as quickly as it opened in 1995. Certainly, the Lord gives and He takes away, especially when the key person within that ministry was very deceptive;

16 – CLEAN AIR AND REAL CHRISTIANITY

the *devil may honor deception,* but *the Lord never will* (1 Corinthians 3:18-20). The third person who really touched my heart was Pastor Julius Muangi. His countenance was shining with joy, and his gentle words were always comforting; he was truly an ambassador for Christ.

Over the years, I had many wonderful meals in his home; his wife certainly was the perfect example of grace. Julius would frequently invite me to the prayer meeting of the AIM, a Baptist-based theology, and he always enjoyed the way I would pray Scripture. One night, we were down at the orphanage praying, and when we walked outside, I thought there was a spotlight shining across the sky, so I looked up and asked, "What is that light?" Julius glanced up and asked me if I had never seen the Milky Way; it was so magnificent, with hundreds of other stars surrounding it, all I could say was, "I have never seen the glory of God like that!"(Psalm 19:1). Julius said, "That is nothing compared to what we will see one day!"

Each year that I went back to Kijabe, I noticed that the visibility was decreasing because of Nairobi's smog drifting up into the Rift Valley area, and I shared my concern with Duncan about that on several occasions. He would pass it off as just being a foggy day; however, in the 4th year, it was so noticeable that one could hardly see the NASA tracking center in the Rift Valley. It reminded me of my childhood days in Greenville, South Carolina, when I could see mountain range after mountain range of the Appalachians. That is no longer possible unless a major storm system has come through, blowing all of the automobile and truck pollution out of the area, but with Interstate Highways 26, 40, 77, and 85, it just takes about 3 days to cover us again with that hydrocarbon haze layer. The same thing was happening in Kenya, with all of the Nairobi auto and truck pollution, the deforestation in that area, and the fact that most people cooked by open fires in their kitchens, as well as burning their trash. They were like frogs in warm water, not realizing that the heat was increasing, resulting in a noticeable decrease in their beautiful visibility.

I even wrote the Prime Minister of Kenya a letter that year, explaining to him what had happened in the San Bernardino Valley in California, which is now virtually a desert; I wrote, "When droughts come, you will lose your crops, then you will lose your animals, and then you will lose your tourists." I received no response, and, unfortunately, they never did anything regarding exhaust emissions in Nairobi, so that letter turned out to be prophetic. I went back in 2008 for Duncan's graduation from dental school in Uganda, and when we drove across the Great Rift Valley to his home in Narok, the massive herds of zebras frequently crossing the road were minimal compared to just 7 years previously!

Now back to some wonderful memories! I vividly remember the day when Bruce took Duncan, Julius, and me to a Masai village, and I was doing extractions in a small bean shed for privacy while Duncan and Julius were sharing the gospel in their native language. A true Masai warrior came to our little facility with his seven wives, 23 children, and a herd of goats. The gum tissue behind his lower wisdom tooth was infected to the point that it was covering the back half of his tooth, and he could not close his teeth together without biting the infected gum tissue. We call that a severe pericoronitis, and it usually requires antibiotic treatment before the tooth can be removed; however, when one is in a primitive area for just 1 day, that option does not exist.

I anesthetized the area completely and removed that wisdom tooth, placed gauze over the extraction site, indicated for him to bite down on the gauze by closing my mouth, and asked him "OK?" with my finger and thumb in a circle. He nodded to me that he understood, walked out into his goat

16 – Clean Air and Real Christianity

herd, cut the neck of one of his goats, collected the blood in a small cup that he had in his pocket, and drank it! I had heard about drinking fresh blood, but I had never seen it, so as I looked away, I saw a zebra and a gazelle off in the distance, realizing that I was certainly not in South Carolina!

About 20 minutes later, I was back inside the little shed working with another patient when this same Masai warrior came to the doorway saying something in his language. I looked around, only to see his hand extended, with fresh blood all over his hand and forearm, so I grabbed a towel, thinking he had cut his hand. In actuality, he was offering me the heart of the goat he had just killed, the best part of the goat, as thanks for what I had done for him; I held out the towel for him to place the heart inside the towel, and he nodded, tapping his teeth together to show me that he could now close his teeth with no problem. I took a quick look inside his mouth and his bleeding from the extraction site had already stopped, as he had placed some type of Masai paste over it.

Duncan told me later that his gesture of appreciation, offering me the best part of his goat, was common practice within the Masai people, and the ladies of that village cooked the heart for me that evening. I have told that story numerous times in my office to various men, and one time had a man ask me, "Can I bring you a chicken liver for my root canal?" We had a good laugh!

On another outing the following year, Pastor Julius took me to an orphanage that was over 2 hours away from Kijabe, on a very rough road. He warned me that it would be a tough ride, and that none of the other visiting dentists was willing to go there. The four Masai ladies who managed that orphanage had told him, "Don't try to tell us about God when our children have to cry themselves to sleep each night with tooth pain." That was all I needed to hear to motivate me, so I

Miracles Can Be Yours

packed up my portable dental unit that I had brought with me, which would allow me to do fillings, as well as Kijabe's field pack for extractions.

As expected, we bounced all around in our vehicle in transit, and arrived at the orphanage at about 10:00 in the morning. Thirty-two children were at that orphanage, and most of their teeth were in a mess because of some sticky sugar candy that visitors had brought by several years before my arrival. Please, if you ever visit an orphanage in a third world country, don't take sugar candy! We set my self-contained portable dental unit under a nice shade tree, hooked it up to a gas generator, and I got to work right away. With just a short break for lunch, I was back extracting teeth and placing white fillings in their front teeth. Fortunately, just before dark, I was able to finish the last child, and all of them were so appreciative. I was thinking about the children, but the Lord was thinking about the ladies who ran that orphanage, and that night, after the children were fed they went to sleep without any crying.

Then Julius and I had a nice chicken dinner, and Julius shared the Gospel in Masai; all four of the ladies gave their hearts to the Lord, and told him, "Now we know there is a God." Isn't it amazing how the Lord works? When we reach out with compassion, *God performs wondrously,* and often we do not give Him the glory He is due. That reminds me of two of my favorite verses: "A generous man will prosper; he who refreshes others will himself be refreshed" (Proverb 11:25) and "Whoever shuts his ears to the cry of the poor, will also cry himself, and not be heard" (Proverbs 21:13). The ride home that night was an exhausting 3 hours, but Julius and I rejoiced the entire way. It really is amazing the number of times I have been thinking about a certain person, or children in an orphanage, but the Lord, *in HIS sovereign plan,* invariably has someone

16 – Clean Air and Real Christianity

else in mind, like the ladies in the orphanage. Yes, His ways are far above ours (Isaiah 55:8)!

Several years later, my dear friend, Pastor Julius, was tragically killed in an auto/bus head-on collision, so I know he went to Paradise quickly. He always had a joyful smile on his face, and I heard from Duncan that when the officials removed his body from the wreckage, he was still smiling! If Julius had any final conscious thoughts, I'm sure they were as glorious as the ones my sweet mom had right before her departure with Jesus's angels. So many things in this world we are not meant to understand, and for our comfort, the Lord says, "It is the glory of God to conceal a matter" (Proverbs 25:2). He just doesn't want us to know everything, for reasons only He knows!

CHAPTER 17
ANOTHER ENGLISH COLONY

If I thought covering several trips to Kenya was going to be like eating an elephant, I guess covering 11 trips to Guyana, South America will be like eating a whale! However, before I proceed with my first bite, please let me back up and tell you how Guyana even entered into the picture, as it is almost a miracle in itself. God can break down any and all barriers whenever He likes, and that is what happened one day in the fall season of 2003 when a previous patient of mine walked into the office with a comment that shocked me. Holding up a cassette tape, she calmly said, "God told me to give this tape to you." In my prideful arrogance, I almost said, "Sure, God told you!" but she never gave me the chance, as she continued on, telling me that it was a message from Jack Deere who was to be the speaker at one of the Morning Star Conferences in Pineville. She said, "I promise you, this will be well worth your time, even if you have to change your schedule, so please be sure to go." Well, I almost dropped in my tracks when she handed me the tape and my nametag for the Prophetic Ministry Conference of Morning Star Church. Then she said, "Please be sure to purchase Jack Deere's book, *Surprised by The Power of The Spirit*; it will be on the book table when you go into Lifespring Church where they are holding the confer-

17 – ANOTHER ENGLISH COLONY

ence." All of this probably took place in less than 30 seconds, and God seared all of it into my mind. Furthermore, with all of those *pleases* and *I promise yous*, I was most intrigued, especially with the SAT 10:35 under my name. Then, with a "Bless you, Dr. Fuller," she turned and left the office. I think that was one of the few times in my life when I have been speechless!

I listened to the tape and really was not impressed by the unenthusiastic delivery by Jack Deere, but it was scripturally a very sound message, so I went to the conference. Arriving about 30 minutes before it started, I bought the book, and was surprised that the church was almost full. Normally, I like sitting near the front when I attend conferences, but that was impossible, so I scrambled over a few people near the back of the auditorium and found a vacant seat between a man about my age and a young boy. Loud praise music was being played by a band, people were excited, and someone kept blowing a strange-sounding horn just a few rows in front of us!

I must have been looking around inquisitively when the man beside me asked, "You aren't used to this, are you?" I told him that I had never seen anything like this before at a church meeting, and asked him what type of horn that was making that strange sound. About that time the lady beside the young boy, who turned out to be his mother, told me it was a shofar, and said that I was going to be really blessed tonight. I thanked her and asked how old her son was; he was 10. Then I asked her what the SAT 10:35 was on my name tag, and she said with excitement, "That is your prophetic ministry time in the other building, for Saturday; be sure not to miss that." The band began blasting loud praise music again, so I just sat quietly until they finished their song. Then the man beside me confirmed the fact that I definitely did not want to miss my Saturday scheduled time. I was trying to take all of this in when the little boy tapped me on the shoulder, saying, "Mister,

Miracles Can Be Yours

God wants you to know that your computer problems will be over tomorrow;" so I asked him how he knew I was having computer problems. He smiled and said he didn't, but that God wanted him to give me that message.

About that time, I felt like I was in a really unusual place, certainly not my home church. Rick Joyner welcomed everyone to the conference, right at 7 o'clock, and the band played some more praise music with some amazing singers accompanying them. Jack Deere had a great message regarding healing, again without much enthusiasm, which I was used to from my home church pulpit, and then they asked people *who needed healing to come forward.* That is when I became a little fearful, so instead of going forward, *I went home*; after all, I had a meeting with the Hank Williams Evangelistic Ministry the following morning, with about a 2 hour drive to get there; and I *certainly didn't need any healing!* Isn't it amazing how we try to rationalize getting away from the presence of God, when we are loaded down with guilt and personally inflicted shame? Please remember, this was the time when, although I was *actively involved* in Christian ministry, I was *still fighting demons and spirits* that I could not even recognize. So what does God do?

After our Hank Williams Evangelistic Ministry board meeting, as I was walking into the restaurant for lunch with our board members, I was listening to my voicemail messages when my mouth must have dropped open. Hank asked me if I had a problem with a patient, and I responded, "No, that was my computer man who just told me that my Ethernet chips were bad from a power surge, and my computer problems are now over." Then I told Hank about the little boy who gave me that message the previous night. That is when Olin Lee, one of our board members, said, "You must have heard that from the Morning Star Conference at Lifespring Church." Then he said that his son, Randy, was the music minister at Lifespring.

17 – ANOTHER ENGLISH COLONY

"Be sure to meet him tonight," he said. We had a nice lunch, and I contemplated all of this on the drive home.

I met Randy Lee that night before the conference started, and told him that I was on the Hank Williams board with his dad, and about the message from the little boy the previous night and confirmation of that today by voicemail. He did not seem surprised at all with the events, encouraged me to go to my prophetic ministry time on Saturday, invited me to come to church there on Sunday, and had to excuse himself to get ready for the conference. A few minutes later, I realized that he was the one from the previous night who could really play the saxophone!

Then Saturday morning rolled around, so I went into their gym area at about 10:30 with my briefcase, and sat in the waiting area. Right at 10:35, a lady with ribbons on her jacket came into the area and called for Noel Fuller. She introduced herself and led me back to a curtained-off area, introducing me to another gentleman and a teenage girl inside a small area where I took a seat facing all three of them. The leader asked me if I had ever had prophetic ministry before, so I told her no, and she explained they were just going to have a short prayer, and let me know what God had revealed to them. I asked her if I could take notes, and she said, "Please do; we normally record these sessions but today we don't have that capability." She must have sensed that I was a little uncomfortable because she asked, "Are you comfortable with this?" I nodded that everything was okay, so they bowed their heads, and the leader led us in a short prayer, asking God to reveal things to them that could benefit me or be uplifting to me. I thought to myself, "Wow, this is going to be good!" Well, I wrote about two sentences of notes as the girl was speaking, before I said, "*Do you know who I am, and where I am going?*" The teenage girl said, "Oh, no, we don't want to know anything," and she continued telling me the details of what was going to happen in a mountainous foreign country soon, and that I would be looking in children's mouths!

Then the leader told me that I needed to be *a more patient man*, closed the 10-minute session with prayer, and asked me what I thought. I think they knew I was totally amazed, as I shared with them that I was going to Kenya the next week, and would probably be working in an orphanage doing dentistry. We all gave praise to the Lord. I found Randy Lee, told him that I was on cloud 9, and that I would see him in the morning for their worship service. As a first-time visitor in their church, they called me forward for prayer before my mission trip! I was blown away again by the fervency of their prayer for a stranger. Needless to say, I was not a stranger for long, because I began attending church there on a regular basis.

Now you know how the Lord was beginning to set me free of my prideful attitude that had essentially covered my sin by searing my conscience, and I had tried to put God in my very small intellectual box that fit my convenience. On the outside I looked okay, but on the inside I was tormented. Please see Chapter 13 regarding how that was resolved. Not long after I returned from Kenya that summer, I met a man at Lifespring Church who was the pastor of Lifespring Ministries in Guyana, South America. I knew in my spirit right away that Balgobind Ragnauth, alias Pastor Lalo, was a special man, as he was giving praise to God for what the Lord had done the previous 10 years in Guyana, sharing how it was Pastor Worley of Lifespring Church in Pineville who gave the initial financial support for him to take his family from New York to Guyana. Since then, Pastor Worley had been a source of encouragement to Pastor Lalo. As the Lord would have it, I was privileged to lead the first mission team from the Pineville Lifespring Church to Lifespring Ministries in Guyana, but that is another chapter.

Chapter 18
The Garden of Eden

How appropriate for this chapter: I just spoke with my good friend Pastor Lalo from Guyana who is a brilliant man with an excellent memory, and he told me that 18 people from Lifespring Church in Pineville, North Carolina went to Guyana, South America in 2004. It was a simple task doing the recruiting, and yet organizing the details of the trip was a complex and challenging undertaking, especially when this was my first such endeavor. However, the Lord was with me every step of the way, and, except for one piece of delayed luggage, everything went without a hitch. We had several excellent prayer sessions before departure, and the excitement level was at an all-time high as we boarded our flight out of Charlotte to Fort Lauderdale, Florida. With our matching, monogrammed, blue polo shirts, we looked like a unified team, and the diversity of our ministry gifts was astounding; only the Lord could have put such a team together.

At the time, Guyana had a charter airline service called Universal Airlines, operating a direct flight from Georgetown to Fort Lauderdale, so we took advantage of their excellent round-trip fare. I remember while we were waiting for our connection, our music minister, Randy Lee, pulled out his saxophone, and put to flight any demonic anxiety spirits at the

Miracles Can Be Yours

Fort Lauderdale airport; we had evangelistic ministry going on right there in the airport. As we boarded the plane, I was distributing a sleeping aid to take with our in-flight meal, so we could sleep on the 5-hour night flight, and one of the big, muscular men on our team asked me, "Is that little pill going to be enough for me?" So I told him to take it right away, and if he wasn't sleepy before the meal, to come and see me, and I would give him another one. When we got to Guyana, he had food dribbled down his shirt, as he was eating and sleeping at the same time. He found out that *little did not mean ineffective*!

Word spread very quickly that Lifespring USA was visiting Lifespring Guyana, and we had various types of ministry taking place: spiritual gifts teaching sessions, evangelistic training, puppet ministry for the children, sports ministry, ladies ministries, and, last but not least, teeth cleaning by our hygienist and extraction of the painful ones by yours truly. The ladies of our team spent each night in a large room above the church, and most of the men were in hammocks on an outside porch. I made the mistake of going to a small building beside the church for a quieter sleeping atmosphere, but the mosquitoes feasted on my exposed shoulder the first night — must have had 30 bites in a 4-square-inch area! Fortunately, I was fairly immune to mosquito bites from my various other South America trips.

We brought with us four duffle bags of shoes to take into the interior to some of the indigenous Guyanese people who did not have shoes; the interior is a rain forest! As I remember, most of the ladies stayed behind in Georgetown while we divided into two different groups of six people, and we took different boats into the interior to deliver the shoes. In my group, we visited an amazing little village, and while I was taking care of a few dental problems, the others were washing people's feet, and fitting them with their first pairs of shoes.

18 – THE GARDEN OF EDEN

I will never forget, as I was finishing up with some teeth extractions, the children were running around with their first pairs of sneakers, and we had three pairs of men's shoes left; three men were waiting to have their feet washed. The pastor of that village had previously told us that he would be last, just in case we didn't have enough shoes to go around; however, the Lord revealed His sovereign power that day, as the last pair of shoes fit him perfectly! Our team was ecstatic, and crying with joy at the same time, and the pastor asked us, "Why are you crying?" Someone on our team responded that it was just a miracle that we had the perfect number of shoes and the right sizes. The pastor said, "We prayed that the Lord would provide for everyone."

Needless to say, Americans from the north learned a great truth that day, as God showed us that we had everything, but weak faith in Christ; whereas, our primitive brothers to the south had nothing, and strong faith in Christ! I instantly had great admiration for the people of Guyana, as my memory took me back to the village in Mexico that had fresh fruit year round, clean air, clean water, and love for each other. Yes, the Guyana village was another Garden of Eden!

On the boat ride back we had numerous encounters with short rain showers, and kept pulling a tarp over our heads, then the sun would come out, followed by another shower. Parrots were flying all around, and monkeys were in the trees on the way out of the mangrove forest right along the Caribbean coast. What an amazing day that we will never forget, and each time I bump into one of our team members in the Charlotte area, he or she invariably says, "Remember when we... in Guyana?" Perhaps that is one reason why I really look forward to going back each year; a trip to Guyana, or Kenya, for that matter, leaves an indelible imprint in the human mind, and a trip to the interior of Guyana opens the door for the

Miracles Can Be Yours

miraculous, which is normal for them. Please let me share just a couple of the miraculous events I have experienced that the Lord has permanently etched into my memory bank.

One afternoon I was inside a small, open-air church, which is the standard design for Guyana, and I was seeing many patients who had come in their little canoes for tooth extractions. Most people in that area made their canoes by hand with their machetes out of cork trees, so there was no problem with buoyancy. The common mode of transportation in the interior of Guyana is by boat or footpath, and there are very few roads for automobile travel. As the afternoon began to turn to evening very quickly, the mosquitoes began to arrive on the scene, and in just minutes it was dark, with literally dozens of mosquitoes buzzing around my lone headlamp for visibility in the mouth. I had six patients anesthetized for extractions, so I knew it was going to be a rough encounter fighting those crazy mosquitoes.

About that time, Pastor Lalo and one of his friends walked into the church, saw my dilemma, and asked me, "How are you working, with all those bugs around?" I told him that I didn't have any bug spray. He saw the waiting patients and said, "Lord, get rid of the bugs, please!" I was thinking to myself, "How in the world is the Lord going to get rid of these mosquitoes?" I was hoping, perhaps, for a breeze to blow through the church, but a squadron of bats flew into that church, and ate all the bugs buzzing around me! In amazement, I said, "Thank you, Lalo," and he said, "NO, thank you, Lord!" I was able to complete the remaining patients without a single nuisance bug buzzing around my head. Yes, the Lord can do exceedingly abundantly beyond all that we can ask or think (Ephesians 3:20), even when it comes to eliminating mosquitoes! The following year I had my portable dental unit set up on a covered dock on a beautiful river, and people would just

18 – THE GARDEN OF EDEN

paddle up to the dock, tie their little canoes down, hop out, and get their dental work done. It was a beautiful afternoon with a nice breeze blowing, and I was really enjoying placing fillings in people's front teeth, rather than extracting them.

I was busy working when I noticed a man carrying a lady in his arms up to our covered area, and he placed her in a hammock, looked at me, and said, "Help, doctor, my wife is dying!" Word had spread very quickly in that area that a doctor had come, and I had probably seen 20 dental patients, so I asked him, "Does she have a bad toothache?" thinking perhaps she was dying with toothache pain. He said, "NO, she is dying; she has not eaten for a week!" I took one look at this semi-comatose lady, and knew right away that we did not have a dental problem. She was burning up with a fever and could not respond to me. Immediately, I got up and turned toward the house where Lalo was ministering, and yelled, "Lalo, I need your help!" He came right down to the dock, put his hands on the lady's shoulders, shook her lightly, and started fervently praying — I mean fervently, very loud! I had my hand on the lady's forehead, and, immediately, her fever left.

Needless to say, I was shocked, as medically, that is virtually impossible. Why are we always surprised when God performs a miracle? Lalo continued praying, and within minutes, this lady regained consciousness, and Lalo told someone to get her some coconut milk and a banana. Within half an hour, this lady got up from the hammock, walked down the dock with her husband, and the two of them paddled their little canoe up the river. No one really seemed surprised at what had happened because that type of activity was fairly commonplace. In fact, Lalo is well known in Guyana as Apostle Ragnauth. I have met several people who fraudulently have *Apostle* before their names, but Lalo can demonstrate the truth of his anointing.

Miracles Can Be Yours

I have had the privilege of returning to Guyana each year since that 2004 trip for the celebration of Lifespring Ministries' anniversary in October. The ministry was founded on October 11, 1992, with 11 people on the porch of a home with borrowed church pews! They now have a beautiful, air-conditioned sanctuary, seating 2,000, as well as a large multipurpose facility, and they are debt free; yes, a modern-day Corinthian church, for out of their poverty, they gave in abundance (2 Corinthians 8:2).

The country at that time had a per capita income of $3,500/year, and 93% of the funds for their church came from the residents of Guyana – that is a financial miracle. Not only do they know how to celebrate what the Lord has done every year through their various outreach ministries to the Hindu and Muslim communities nearby, but they know how to love each other, and, last but not least, they know how to cook up some fantastic food to fill the tummies of 2,000+ joyous souls during their celebration. I have taken Pam with me on two separate occasions, Easter and their October Anniversary Celebration. She, too, was amazed by the fact that they have a deep love for not only each other but for our family as well. That is why Lifespring Ministries in Guyana has now expanded throughout the interior, Suriname, Brazil, and will soon be planting another root of Jesse, ironically back in New York, where Lalo, his beautiful wife Pauline, and their little girl, Melissa, left their American dream back in 1992 to obey God's vision for them. They also have two amazing sons, Joshua and Aaron, who were born in Guyana, and are now going to college in Orlando. I look forward to seeing what the Lord is going to do in and through them until Jesus returns, perhaps within my lifetime!

However, the real reason I go back is because I love a man called Lalo, just like I loved Julius in Kenya, who is re-

18 – The Garden of Eden

ceiving his reward right now along with the great cloud of witnesses in Paradise. I'll have to put my pastor, Ken Watson, right up there with Lalo and Julius, because all of them have demonstrated an unquenchable love for Jesus, and every time I am around them, some of that love transfers over to me. I guess that is why the disciples loved Jesus so much; what an amazing transfer that must have been! Just think: One day we will be able to look into the eyes of perfect love, and when that happens we will actually be like Him. What a glorious day that will be!

Chapter 19
Rainy Nights

You may recall, back in Chapter 16, that I had the privilege of going back to Kenya in 2008 for the graduation ceremony of my dear friend Duncan Odupoy. He was to be the first Masai dentist in Kenya, so it was to be a very special occasion. We rented a seven-passenger van and made the drive from his home in Narok, Kenya to Kampala, Uganda, all 8 hours' worth! This trip used to take Duncan 14 hours by bus from Nairobi, Kenya, and he made that trip many times over his 5 years at dental school. The scenery changes were absolutely magnificent, and I was really surprised that the roads were actually very good, as it was a well-traveled highway, necessitating excellent roads.

The Narok area was suffering from a severe drought, and they had lost their entire maize crop, but as we entered into the mountainous areas and the lush tea farms of Kenya, everything was green. Then we crossed the equator and entered into Uganda where the source of the Nile River is located. This is actually a huge swampy plain, and then it was a steady uphill climb into the beautiful forests of Uganda. Duncan's graduation ceremony was a very colorful spectacle, and he was honored as one of the top graduates in his class, which did not

19 – RAINY NIGHTS

surprise me in the least. Then early the next morning, it was seven tired individuals back into the van for the ride home. I could tell Duncan's father was extremely discouraged because of the drought, and he had lost several of his livestock. Each day he had to walk his cows, sheep, and goats for over a mile to a little stream where he would water them and then walk them back to his farm. Their cistern that held the rain water for their personal consumption was almost dry.

Duncan's mom fixed us a wonderful meal that evening, and after the meal I was really surprised when I walked into their kitchen, which was a room detached from the remainder of their modest home. The kitchen was probably 15 by 15 feet, and it was completely black from the smoke of an open fire which was essentially their stove. Most of the Kenyan people cooked over open fires and had small ovens that were heated with wood fires as well. That evening we watched the inauguration of President Obama on their small television. There were fireworks in abundance all around Narok in celebration of that event. Due to the severe drought there was very little vegetation and the large maize fields were just bare dirt, even though they were in the middle of their rainy season. Rain clouds would form each evening but there would be no rain, and depression was running at a high level.

The Lord lay on my heart in a very profound way to pray for rain, so I opened a little book that Pastor Lalo had given me the previous year, and I asked Duncan's father if I could read a portion of it to their family. The book was Cindy Trimm's *The Rules of Engagement*, and it contained a very powerful prayer covering just about every aspect of blessing. I had never been much for reading prayer, but for some reason the Holy Spirit just wanted me to go there. As I read this almost 20-minute prayer, I added specific emphasis regarding rain for Narok,

Miracles Can Be Yours

so they could prepare their soil for a very critical planting for their maize crop. Then I gave thanks to the Lord for what He was going to do, closing in the powerful name of Jesus.

Maize was their primary cash crop for that entire area, and Duncan's father had shared with me how critical it was for them to have a successful planting within the next few weeks. I remember him asking me after our prayer, "You really think it is going to rain, don't you?" I said, "I really do because it is not a want but a need." Then I encouraged all of them to be in agreement with me, and give thanks to the Lord for what He was going to do that night. The clouds were there; they just needed to reach the dew point. So we had a prayer, thanking the Lord for Duncan's graduation, the wonderful meal, and the rain; all of us were in agreement with an attitude of praise!

I had learned over the years that agreement is a very powerful force; in fact, God says when you pray in accordance with My will, you can thank Me for having received it (Mark 11:24). Not surprisingly, that very night we heard the beautiful sound of rain hitting the tin roof of Duncan's house, and the next morning their cistern was almost full. Needless to say, Duncan's father was absolutely ecstatic. Quite frequently, I wear the beautiful belt that Duncan's dad made me as a memento for that trip, and his mother made me a beautiful Masai celebration outfit, that I have worn on numerous occasions of celebration here in the US. Lord willing, perhaps one day I will be back for a visit to see Duncan's precious family.

Now let's take an excursion over the Atlantic Ocean to the continent of South America. I was in the forty-bed hospital at Santa Rosa, deep in the interior of Guyana. This particular trip I had gone into the interior by myself, just to do some dentistry; Lalo had always gone with me before, but he was making preparations for the celebration service. Even though that area is in the middle of a rainforest, for 2 WEEKS there

19 – Rainy Nights

had been no rain, and the main hospital cistern was empty. The physician was having to go to the kitchen area, as it had a larger cistern, to get a bucket of water for the delivery of babies. I was there to do some dentistry, but that was impossible with no water, so I was making the most of my time, passing little mini Bibles out to the patients in the hospital.

The hospital's head nurse who was Hindu apparently got word of my activity, and asked me who I was. I pointed to the Dr. Fuller name tag on my jacket, and told her that I was a dentist, but that we could not operate the clinic without water. She said, "I don't have any paperwork on you; I don't want you in my hospital." I calmly told her that I understood, and I would go outside and pray for rain. She said rather abruptly, "You are going to do what?" So I responded, "You need rain, so I am going to pray for rain." I started to tell her what had happened in Kenya, but she said, "You are crazy," as she turned and walked away. So I gathered up my belongings from the dental clinic, went outside, sat under a beautiful mango tree, and began having an awesome prayer time with the Holy Spirit right beside me.

As I was on my way back to the little guest cottage where I was staying, I bumped into a man named Johnny who operated the motor boat ride to and from a town named Charity which was about 2 hours away. It was an awesome trip, zooming through a large plain of marsh grass in a narrow, curving stream, winding through an amazing forest, across an ocean bay, and then up another river filled with coconut husks. I had gotten to know Johnny pretty well from previous trips into the interior. When I told him what had happened at the hospital, he just smiled with that big Christian grin of his, and said, "I'll be praying with you for rain, too; we sure need it" (Mark 11:24). I thanked him, pointed up to the beautiful blue sky, and said, "In agreement, gonna rain tonight!" and then took

Miracles Can Be Yours

a nice stroll over the little bridge that crossed the river, and walked about a mile to the guest cottage.

The generator for the town electricity turns off at about 7 o'clock each evening, 1 hour after sunset, so I was getting ready for bed when I saw a flash of light, and heard a boom. At first I thought maybe something had happened to the large generator, but the lights were still on, so I walked outside to see what was going on. A few minutes later Johnny rode up on his motor scooter, hopped off, and said, "Did you hear that?" I told him I had seen a flash of light and heard a boom that sounded like thunder, and he said, "We don't have thunder here." About that time a flash of lightning shot across the sky with a big boom of thunder just a few seconds later. I told Johnny, "That's what we call heat lightning in the US," and about that time three or four more streaks of lightning flew across the sky, followed by thunderous booms.

It was one of the most awesome things I have ever seen! It was not heat lightning; they were thunderbolts going across the sky, and it went on for several minutes. The lightning was not coming to the ground, just streaking across the sky (Psalm 18:14, 144:6). Of course, that was followed by almost torrential rain. Johnny said he had never seen anything like that, and he had been living in that area for almost 50 years. The next morning, I went by the hospital to see the nurse, but she did not want to see me; the hospital cistern was overflowing, as it was still raining!

I spoke at the two schools in that area that day, talking about the miracle of the previous night, and the five necessities for good health: proper nutrition, enough water for ones' body weight, adequate sleep, essential exercise, and, last but not least, spiritual nutrition each day. Then I shared the Gospel message, and many of the predominantly Hindu students came forward to receive Christ. Returning back to the hospital

19 – RAINY NIGHTS

that afternoon to see their head nurse, I received the word that she was busy. Early the next morning, I went down to get on the boat back to civilization, and Johnny had a huge smile on his face. He asked me if I had seen the nurse, so I told him, "No, she was busy." He said, "She knows!"

When I got back to Georgetown, Lalo was at the dock to pick me up. I had lost my hat on the 40-mile-per-hour boat ride, and had wrapped some clothing around my head to prevent sunburn, so he did not recognize me until I hugged him. We had a great visit as he drove back to his home, and I shared with Lalo what had happened at Santa Rosa. He said, "Even we could see that lightning up the coast, and I wondered what was going on; to God be the glory!" Needless to say, we had an awesome Celebration Service that year, as I shared what happened with the congregation. Truly, we are "set free by the blood of the Lamb, and the power of our testimony" (Revelation 12:11).

On subsequent trips, whenever I see Johnny, he beams with his huge smile, and points to the sky! Yes, the Lord can still take ordinary people, and do extraordinary things when we come in agreement through prayer and trust Him for His perfect timing. Sometimes He says, "No" and sometimes He says, "Wait," but sometimes He says, "Watch this!" Johnny and I will never forget His awesome display of glory that evening. Lord willing, next time I go back to Santa Rosa, I'm going to see if that nurse is still at the hospital; I'm sure she will remember this "Crazy Man."

Chapter 20
How About You?

If you are like some people, myself included, and jump to the back of the book, especially if it sounds interesting, that is not the best way to read this one! However, if you are rushed, like many in our crazy state of business, please go to Chapter 8 first, and if you are struggling with victory in your spiritual walk or freedom from guilt, please go to Chapter 13. I have tried to paint a picture of our Sovereign Lord in the first seven chapters, so if you don't *know His sovereign power*, please start with Chapter 1, and those will be preparatory for the journey with me. Please be patient, as this is a 35-year marathon run, done with somewhat of a sprint. Lord willing, it will be completed by Easter, 2016; how appropriate!

I have certainly been very transparent for the past 19 chapters, and my prayer is that you have been encouraged, stretched, challenged, and perhaps convicted on occasion, regarding your own walk, or lack thereof, with the Lord. Hopefully, you know by now that for 17 years *following my salvation encounter with Christ*, I was subtly deceived by that crafty, conniving enemy and his host of demonic spirits, as well as the world system that I could not let go of with any consistency. I was lying to myself and others regarding my bondage to ra-

20 – HOW ABOUT YOU?

tionalized sins; please know that your accountability is only as effective as your honesty.

Yes, we are to confess our sin to one another, but how often does that take place in Christian circles? Our human nature is to hide our sins, but who do we think we are fooling when we do that? Unfortunately, it is just me, myself, and I – the unholy trinity! Sanctification is certainly a process, but I know many people who purposefully delay that process, and some of them have a seared conscience (1 Timothy 4:2). They have not lost their salvation, BUT they have certainly lost their joy, and true FREEDOM in one's mind is a distant mirage. The desire to witness for Christ or to participate in the Great Commission is non-existent, and unfortunately, this is the majority.

If you have fallen into *the bondage of rationalized sin*, I pray that the Holy Spirit will do *whatever it takes* to get your attention for *thorough and effective repentance* before you fall and lose your witness. That may sound a little harsh, but the last thing we need in these final days is more *lukewarm* (Revelation 3: 16) churchians who claim to be Christians. Paul said, "May it never be!" (Romans 6:15), and he knew that sin was and would be a constant battle throughout life, but we certainly don't need to embrace sin like we do now. My pastor says, "If we can do wrong and not feel wrong, then something is wrong." He also reminds us that we can never attain perfection, but as we pursue it, we can attain excellence.

You may not know that only TWO of the SEVEN churches made the commendation of Christ (Revelation 3) and those types of churches exist today; which one do you belong to, or attend, or are you a couch Christian? If Lucifer could deceive one third of the host of heaven, I feel certain that he can deceive two thirds of the people on earth. Your relationship with

Miracles Can Be Yours

Christ may be personal, but is it private? I pray not! I think our *entitlement mentality* today has fed the convenient, easy-living theology, which eliminates the books of Peter, and our *elitism mentality* feeds the prosperity gospel theology. Like I said before, most of us have bought the C/R switch: instead of confession and repentance, we have been taught, and learned with expertise, how to compromise and rationalize, so we put more money in the plate to *feel good*, and feed the *economic enterprise of the false church*. Perhaps our offering is an abomination to the TRUE GOD. Please check out "abomination" in Proverbs; you may be surprised that the wisest man who ever lived uses that term frequently; or do you want to *remain comfortable in your sin?!*

If your foundation is not *in Christ* (Ephesians 1:3), perhaps you should review Chapter 8 because that is the starting point for any victorious walk in life. A good test to see where you stand is really simple: *Are you producing fruit, or are you at least trying?* If you don't even know what that means, you may be headed to the trash pile of dead branches (John 15:5-6). Some people have been blessed with excess money, and think they are fairly secure with all of the world's pleasures, but "what does it profit a man to gain the whole world yet lose his soul?" (Matthew 16:26; Mark 8:36; Luke 9:25).

So if you find yourself in a very secure financial position, you may want to do a word study on *money or wealth* in Proverbs to find out if your blessing is from the Lord, because *it may be from the devil himself.* Or if you think you have a solid foundation in Christ, and yet you are striving or trying to earn favor with God, then you certainly are on the wrong rocky road of religious works, and numerous denominations will take you down that path of total frustration. We can never earn, nor do we deserve right standing with God; only Christ can secure

20 – HOW ABOUT YOU?

that for us, and Jesus has already *completed the task with perfection*. He is, still present tense, our sacrificial lamb, and He said, "It is finished" (John 19:13); that means completed forever!

So if you think or believe that *any additional offering* is necessary for you to be acceptable or right with God, then you have been deceived. However, if you know for certain that you are standing on solid ground, in the person of Jesus Christ, and you know that you will be in the clouds one day with the saints, BUT you find yourself lacking in the realm of *joy and total freedom*, or if specific sins *keep popping up* in your mind or in your actions, perhaps you might want to review Chapter 13. I certainly don't have all of the answers, but Lord willing, I may be able to point you in the right direction to secure your FREEDOM. If you would like to contact a non-denominational ministry that will certainly help you with that glorious word (Freedom), I'd recommend 3: *www.ransomedheart.com*, *www.refugeranch.info*, or *www.zoweh.org*. I have personally been involved with all of them, and would like to assure you, you WILL be blessed with their events. Ransomed Heart is now international, and the latter two are based out of the Carolinas. In the USA. Yes, FREEDOM, like most things, is a choice; do you prefer bondage or freedom? Unfortunately, religion is bondage, but true Christianity is freedom. If you prefer religion, there are hundreds from which to choose. Please don't get into the trap of prideful tradition that had me snared for years!

I like to consider the Great Commission (Matthew 28:18-20) *The Final Command of Christ*, and if we truly know Him, we will love Him, and we WILL obey Him, out of a *heart of gratitude* for what He has already done on the cross; what an amazing transaction took place there – His perfection for our sin! When Jesus said, "Go," that word means, "as you go, or wherever you go," and may I please add "continue to go;" yes, obedience is

MIRACLES CAN BE YOURS

not *just a one-time event*. My family has received many amazing blessings, as I have obeyed His initial call to me, on my first mission trip, to be involved in missions, and, by His grace, I have been able to continue that obedience over the years.

Yes, obedience is certainly more important than sacrifice (1 Samuel 15:22). My brother Calvin certainly received a blessing from the Lord for his obedience to God's call on his first mission trip, when he met his soul mate; they were married a year later on my birthday. I wrote them a little poem, which I read at their wedding. I'll include that at the end of this chapter. SO, the question is: When are you going to obey, and make YOUR vacation time a time of service for Jesus? You certainly don't have to go across the ocean, but have you ever set a specific amount of time aside *to pray about your involvement in some type of mission work?* You won't regret it! We can all tell other people just who Jesus is; most people in the world certainly don't know that He is the one who made the universe! (Colossians 1:16; Hebrews 1:2).

So here's to your obedience to the final words of the greatest theologian of all time, Paul, who said, "Fix your thoughts on what is true, honorable, right, pure, lovely, and admirable. Think about things that are excellent and worthy of praise" (Philippians 4:8). Another good test is to see if your thoughts and actions line up with TRUE FRUIT, "the fruit of the spirit is love, joy, peace, patience, kindness, goodness, faithfulness, gentleness, and self-control" (Galatians 5:22). Certainly, we have too much FALSE fruit for sale these days. You know the final words of Jesus. So, one of my final words to you is very simple; it is God's word: "OBEY!"

If you would like to peruse a very effective victory prayer, compliments of Cindy Trimm's *The Rules of Engagement* which I have modified slightly as a shorter version (and it is a great Bible study lesson, too), it follows. SO, here's to getting rid of

20 – How About You?

the demonically deceptive trash in the bottom of your cup so God can fill it with His love, and, more importantly, so your prayer won't be an abomination to HIM (Proverbs 28:9). Please, I encourage you, *empty your cup of tarnished sins through specific, truthful confession and repentance*. Once again, a "forgive my shortcomings" is not very sincere or effective! May the Lord bless you and keep you, as you obey (1 John 1:9), and may I see you in the sky one glorious day (1 Thessalonians 4:16).

Please see the following prayer:

Freedom and Victory!
Pray with someone else OUT LOUD; yes, agreement is powerful:

We come in the name of the resurrected Jesus, whose we are and whom we serve, "that at the name of Jesus every knee should bow, of things in heaven, and things in earth, and things under the earth; and that every tongue should confess that Jesus Christ is Lord" (Phil 2:10-11; Psm 82). We affect and enforce God's original plans and purposes over and against the plans and purposes of Satan, and we say "Lord, please rebuke him" (Dan. 6). We decree and declare that in this battle, no intrinsic (internal) or extrinsic (external) weapon, be it emotional, financial, social, physical, psychological, interpersonal, spiritual, or organizational formed against us shall prosper (1Sam 17:47; Isa 54:17; Jer 51:20; Jn 14:30; 2Cor 7:5; Eph 4:27).

We place upon ourselves the armor of truth to cover our loins, the breastplate of righteousness to cover our hearts, the gospel of peace to cover our feet, the shield of faith to cover our bodies, and the helmet of salvation to cover our heads; we use effectively the sword of the Spirit which is the "appropriate spoken Word of God," and pray at all times in the Spirit (Eph 6:14-18). We put on the Lord Jesus Christ (Rom 13:14), His robe of righteousness (Isa 61:10), and give thanks that the glory of God is our rear guard (Isa 58:8).

MIRACLES CAN BE YOURS

We decree and declare that the weapons of our warfare are not carnal but mighty through God, (1 Sam 17:45; Rom 13:12; 2 Cor 10:3-6) as we pull down strongholds and cast down vain imaginations and every high thing that lifts itself against the knowledge of Jesus Christ. Our thoughts are now subject to the Lordship of Christ (Isa 14:13-14; Ezek 28:2; 2Cor 10:5). We speak that God's anointing destroys every yoke in our lives, our bodies, and that our souls function according to divine systems of protocol (1 Cor 9:27, 14:40). We bind every diabolical sanction, subverting activity, injunction, directive, mandate, or order that opposes the will of the Lord concerning our lives, ministries, and families (Matt 18:18).

We dispossess master spirits and employ Michael, other archangels, and the angelic host to handle any satanic contentions, disputes, strivings, and resistance concerning this injunction (2 Kings 7:5-7; 2 Chron 32:21; Dan 3:24-25, 6:22,10:13; Psm 91:11, 103:20; Heb 1:14). We declare successful divine and angelic undertaking, undergirding, reinforcements, and assistance. According to Your Word in Ps 103:20, angels now "excel in strength" to marshal and protect our personage, property, and possessions (2 Kings 6:17; Dan 3:15-30; Acts 12:1-10). Jehovah-Gibbor, please contend with those who contend with us, and fight against those who fight against us. Let terror strike the hearts of our enemies and cause their hearts to fail. We announce that it is YOU who has blessed us, and it is YOU who empowers us. It is not by our might, nor by our power, but by the Spirit of the Lord, for when the enemy comes in like a flood, Your Spirit lifts up a standard against him (Ex15:3; Deut 32:41-42; Psm 7:13, 18:29-50, 35:1-8, 144:5-7; Isa 42:13-14, 59:16-19).

We resist satanic contentions, intentions, and negotiations concerning our lives and our souls, and we superimpose prophetic purpose and Divine destiny over and against all

20 – How About You?

activities and opposing forces that are contrary to the will of God in Christ Jesus concerning our lives (1 Sam 1:1-8; 1Kings 22:1-23; 1 Chron 21:1-2; Job 1-7-12, 3:25; Jude 1:9). We bind satanic harassment and rebuke satanic concentrations (2 Sam 11:1-2). We bring to a halt and prohibit any satanic surveillance (1 Sam 18; Matt 26:4; Mark 11:18; Luke 6:11; Acts 16:16-19). We lift false burdens and remove feelings of heaviness, oppression, and depression. We cast them upon the Lord who sustains.

We shall not be moved (Psm 12:5, 54:2, 55:22; Isa 10:27, 61:3; Matt 11:28-30; Jn 14:1). We decree and declare that by the anointing, anything that may block the fulfillment of God's original plan and purpose in our lives is broken. We are liberated from generational/satanic/demonic alliances, allegiances, soul ties, spirits of inheritance, and curses. We sever them by the sword of the Lord, the blood of Christ, and the Spirit. We are free from any and all influences passed down from one generation to another – biologically, socially, emotionally, physically, psychologically, physiologically, spiritually, or by any other channel unknown to us but known to God.

We resist every spirit that acts as a gatekeeper or a doorkeeper to our souls, and we renounce any further conscious or unconscious alliance, association, or covenant. We open ourselves to Divine deliverance. Father, have your way now! Perfect those things concerning us (Deut 5:9, 7:8-9; Eccl 7:26; Isa 61:1; Acts 8:9-13; Gal 5:1; 1 Thes 5:23-24; 2 Tim 2:25). We decree that a prayer shield, the anointing, fire walls, smoke screens, and the bloodline of Christ form hedges of protection around us, and hide us from the scourge of the enemy and any demonic personalities, making it difficult, if not impossible, for them to track or trace us in the realm of the spirit. There shall be no penetrations or perforations to these hedges of protection (Ex 12:13; Job 1:7-10; Ps 91; Zech 2:5).

Miracles Can Be Yours

We put a halt to all distractive, disturbing, or destructive measures. For this reason was the Son of God made manifest, that He would destroy the works of the enemy (John 2:15-17; Acts 16:16-19; 1 John 3:8). We prohibit the alteration or changing of any times or laws concerning our lives, ministries, or the lives of our families. We move in accordance with the movements of God (Dan 6:1-15, 7:15-27). We decree that this day we operate according to God's divine timetable, and that God's agenda is our agenda. We are not our own, we have been bought with a price. We submit ourselves to Christ alone, and we declare that like Jesus, "we come in the volume of the book it is written of us" (Ps 40:7, 139:16; 1 Cor 7:23; James 4:7).

We overrule and overthrow, according to Isaiah 54:17, ill-spoken words, ill wishes, enchantments, divinations, spells, hexes, curses, witchcraft prayers, and every idle word spoken contrary to God's original plans and purposes. We come against falsehoods, slander, speculation, accusation, misrepresentation, and character assassination. Father, please cause the heavens to come down with divine blessing, and prohibit the accuser of the brethren from operating or influencing the soul of anyone who comes in contact with us (1 Kings 21:1-16; Psm 144:5-7; Rev 12:10).

We reverse the effect of any stigmas and declare that divine favor, grace, honor, and well wishes now replace any and all negative feelings, perceptions, and thoughts concerning ourselves, our families, and the work and ministries that we are called to accomplish. We decree that wisdom is our counselor, the Holy Spirit is our consultant, and Jesus Christ is our advocate. God, El Elyon, our only judge has declared and we, therefore, establish that our officers are peace, our exactors righteousness, our walls salvation, and our gates praise (Gen 47:27; Isa 60:17-18).

20 – HOW ABOUT YOU?

We are daily loaded with benefits, and we declare success and progress in Jesus' name, as the Kingdom of Heaven rules and reigns (Psm 68:19; 2 Cor 2:14; Rev 11:15). We decree that the laws that govern this prayer and all spiritual warfare strategies and tactics are binding by the Word, the blood, and the Spirit, and that every spirit released from their diabolical assignment now becomes a part of the footstool of Jesus, as we seal this prayer in His powerful name. Amen! (1 John 5:7-8; Ps 110:1)

ANN AND CALVIN – DEC 19, 2009

My big brother went on a mission trip to Mexico

I told him if he did he would be blessed fo show

Sure enough, reading a book on the porch

Out walks the lady who would light his torch

They start talking and the next thing you know

Calvin is driving to Raleigh each day for mow

So we fast forward to the date right above

Ann down the aisle, no one will have to shove

Yes, true love has a mighty strong attraction

And in Italy they will certainly go into action

Eatin' all kinds of good food and lookin' at places

And everyone will see the love on their faces

So here's to that perfect love that only Jesus gives

May it flow through their lives as each of them lives

In obedience to the One who brought them together

Knowing that the Lord will keep them safe forever

So into His hands we commit them today

Asking that by faith in heaven they will stay

Addendum for Future Contemplation

For several years I have been telling people: "We are living in the most exciting times in the history of the Earth because so much is going to happen so fast." I am certainly no theologian, but most Biblical scholars agree that we are in the latter days. Perhaps one of the most disconcerting tendencies that I have witnessed over the past 36 years of foreign mission trips is not only a worldwide increase in the elitist mentality, but also the entitlement attitude, and both of them have their root in greed. Conveniently, greed has a very simple password "MORE"; and fortunately, there is also a simple solution, "REPENT". However, most people do not know the true meaning of repent, nor does the church, and that is why this cycle of elitism/entitlement is perpetuated. It does not matter what top level professions in the world, or the poorest of third world countries, when any segment becomes selfish, an opposite one becomes jealous; hence, the cycle of confusion begins, and it has NO financial barriers. That is not my idea, but my brother in the Lord, James, by the inspiration of the Holy Spirit, wrote "Where there is selfish ambition and bitter jealousy, there is disorder and every evil thing." (James 3:16) That simple statement certainly clarifies the downward spiral of our culture since the loss of the human heart in the Garden

Addendum for Future Contemplation

of Eden, and our degradation will continue to expand into an unsustainable level of greed, unless the Lord intervenes. My prayer is that the Lord will bring a final revival of tsunami proportion that will lead to repentance; that is the solution with the most promising results.

The Lord will certainly find all of His lost sheep, and Wycliffe Bible Translators is soon to have His glorious Word available to the heart language of every tribe and tongue. Yes, be encouraged, He will have His Word circulated in accordance with His perfect time plan, and we may have the privilege of witnessing the amazing event of His return. What fabulous days will His people have when they hear, "Well done, my good and faithful servants." I pray that you will be in that remnant of saints on the earth when He returns, and you will receive an amazing reward. Once again, our motivation to be a faithful servant should be out of gratitude for what Christ did for us on the cross; we cannot comprehend the agony that He endured before and on the cross, nor can we comprehend His amazing love that would be willing to exchange His perfection for our sin. The Lord literally experienced Hell for us! Are you ready to be a prayer warrior and participate in the final harvest of souls into His Kingdom. PLEASE, let's intensify our prayer life and our service to the Lord as His true disciples should.

No one knows WHEN the trumpet will sound, but one thing, for sure, is when it does sound, everything is going to happen very FAST. When God says something, we can certainly hang our hats on that, and in Revelation Chapter 18, on 3 occasions John, by inspiration of the Holy Spirit, talks about how quickly Babylon will come to an end - ONE hour! Please take or make the time to read the entire chapter; it is fascinating. The mystery Babylon that He is referring to may just be the United States! It certainly was not the Babylon of old, as it had no sea ports.

Miracles Can Be Yours

My dear Pastor Lalo in Guyana has been doing extensive study on asteroids; he believes there are 17 just awaiting God's command to come to the earth, and if one hits the Atlantic Ocean it will take less than an hour to take out the East Coast of the United States with a horrific tsunami, and the same effect would be efficacious for the West Coast if one were to hit the Pacific Ocean. Furthermore, if one were to hit the center of the United States, it would create a tremendous explosion, and what would come back down to our beautiful country would be fire and brimstone. That is probably what took out Sodom and Gomorrah and perhaps Nineveh, to their surprise!

Or perhaps the weapon of indignation spoken of by Daniel the Prophet could very well be a nuclear bomb on a satellite 20 miles over the US, which would cause an immediate power failure of virtually every source, even our cars and cell phones! Please do your own research on the electromagnetic pulse (EMP). So we are indeed living in very exciting and precarious times, and people all around the world need to be ready for the dreadful Day of the Lord. (There are numerous Scripture references on that so PLEASE, do your own study on that.) Are you ready for that day? Chapter 20 of Revelation describes the Glorious return of Christ. He will be streaking through the sky like lightning on his white horse (Matthew 24:27). He won't be coming as Savior this time; He will be coming as judge, and ultimately, HIS proclamation will be FINAL. The army of saints who will rule with Jesus will have two-edged swords in their hands to execute the vengeance of the Lord... this honor have all the saints. Please read the last four verses of Psalm 149. Praise the Lord.

Certainly by now you know that I stand firmly on the Word of God, and I find it very interesting, in TWO different identical verses, that Solomon wrote, by inspiration of the Holy Spirit, "A prudent man foresees evil and hides himself, but the

Addendum for Future Contemplation

simple pass on and are punished" (Proverbs 22:3, 27:12). So as the Day of the Lord approaches, you may want to consider a safe haven, with a hand pump on your well – just wise food for thought if you want to persevere to the end. Furthermore, Solomon's final conclusion is found in Ecclesiastes 12:13,14 if you would like to check that out. It is very clear; in fact, the entire book is phenomenal. I pray that you will be one of those who persevere to the end, and will be saved (Matthew 24:13). Perhaps we all need to diligently confess our sins to people we can trust, be more fervent and effective in our prayer life, while we strive for righteousness (James 5:16). Yes, we may not attain it, but we certainly should be striving for it; please remember that the C/R switch (Chapter 13) never produces JOY. So here's to a glorious meeting with you in the sky, as we look forward to that day! What an awesome day that will be when we look into the eyes of perfect love and hear Jesus say, "Well done, my good and faithful servant"... "Enter into my rest." (There are numerous references on that.) Unfortunately, most people will hear their final judgment as He says, "Depart from me, for I never knew you" (Matthew 7:21-23). Then they will know that He is truly Lord of Lords and King of Kings, and they will all bow their knees to him and proclaim that He is Lord (Romans 14:11; Philippians 2:10). Which group will you be in? "There is a narrow road which leads to life, and few are on it" (Matthew 7:14). Furthermore, faith without works is dead (James 2:14-26). Please don't misunderstand me, good works will NEVER get you to heaven, Jesus is the ONLY one who can and already has secured that for people who know Him and love Him, but good works with the right motive to honor Christ will produce rewards now and in the future. Those rewards may not be financial, so please do NOT look for that type of blessing necessarily. For certain, His ways are not our ways (Isaiah 55:8-9).

Miracles Can Be Yours

Finally, our position in Christ certainly determines our direction, and our obedience to His call, which is our choice, will determine the rewards at our final destination, so please review the end of Chapter 8 if you are not firmly positioned in Christ. I could share about more miracles that I have personally experienced in primitive areas where true belief in Christ predominates, but what God's remaining loyal ones need is more conviction by the Holy Spirit, more repentance, and more commitment to obedience by those who truly love Christ, so please ask for that conviction. Yes, IF my people, who are called by MY name would (1) humble themselves, (2) confess their sins, (3) repent…, and (4) pray…, THEN! He would HEAL… You know, the God who is the same yesterday, today, and forever still does that, it is easy for Him! Simple formula, isn't it? Do you know those references? One is old testament, and one is new!

However, most of us continue to follow the world system and entertain ourselves into oblivion, and as long as we FEEL good, we think we are OK. I personally have seen on several occasions, when TV access creeps into primitive areas, contentment decreases and crime increases. Yes, the US exports over 65% of the world's pornography, and our mother country, England, is #2! We may very well be the Whore of Babylon! Alcohol will destroy the brain, but porn will destroy the soul – mind, will, and emotions – so if that demonic spirit – and porn is a spirit – contaminates your mind's eye, please expose it to God's light immediately, before it becomes a stronghold of denial, and you say, "I'm FINE!" The simple truth is that what you feed will grow! Ironically, denial is also a spirit, and as long as it is in your mind, a verbal wound can never be healed, nor can another Kingdom of Darkness spirit be uncovered. Hebrews 12:1-2 AND Romans 12:1-2 are a much better solution. So please STUDY the glorious, mirac-

Addendum for Future Contemplation

ulous Word of God for yourself and obey; you may just see some miracles – they can be yours, too! Unfortunately, most people would prefer to add another pill to their regimen from our pharmaceutical gurus! As always, the choice is yours.

Please see our website shown on the back cover if you are a more visual person; reading allows people the stimulating experience of creating their own word pictures, but sometimes a picture is worth a thousand words; Lord willing, we will have a photo gallery and some Godly videos there. If this addendum resonates with you, we would appreciate your prayers; the enemy is always there to confuse, deceive, deny, distort, distract, and even kill. Yes, the spirits of the kingdom of darkness are always there, BUT the Kingdom of Light will shine brighter one day over ALL of the earth, and darkness will be extinguished forever. Praise God for the blood of Christ, and the prayers of the saints.